Philosophical Mysteries

SUNY Series in Systematic Philosophy
Robert C. Neville, Editor

Whether systematic philosophies are intended as true pictures of the world, as hypotheses, as the dialectic of history, or as heuristic devices for relating rationally to a multitude of things, they each constitute articulated ways by which experience can be ordered, and as such they are contributions to culture. One does not have to choose between Plato and Aristotle to appreciate that Western civilization is enriched by the Platonic as well as Aristotelian ways of seeing things.

The term "systematic philosophy" can be applied to any philosophical enterprise that functions with a perspective from which everything can be addressed. Sometimes this takes the form of an attempt to spell out the basic features of things in a system. Other times it means the examination of a limited subject from the many angles of a context formed by a systematic perspective. In either case systematic philosophy takes explicit or implicit responsibility for the assessment of its unifying perspective and for what is seen from it. The styles of philosophy according to which systematic philosophy can be practiced are as diverse as the achievements of the great philosophers in history, and doubtless new styles are needed for our time.

Yet systematic philosophy has not been a popular approach during this century of philosophical professionalism. It is the purpose of this series to stimulate and publish new systematic works employing the techniques and advances in philosophical reflection made during this century. The series is committed to no philosophical school or doctrine, nor to any limited style of systematic thinking. Whether the systematic achievements of previous centuries can be equalled in the 20th depends on the emergence of forms of systematic philosophy appropriate to our times. The current resurgence of interest in the project deserves the cultivation it may receive from the SUNY Series in Systematic Philosophy.

Philosophical Mysteries

Stephen David Ross

State University of New York Press

Albany

Published by
State University of New York Press, Albany

© 1981 State University of New York

For information, address State University of New York
Press, State University Plaza, Albany, N.Y,, 12246

Library of Congress Cataloging in Publication Data

Ross, Stephen David.
   Philosophical mysteries.

   Bibliography: p.
   Includes index.
   1. Philosophy.   2. Ontology.   3. Metaphysics.
I. Title.
B53.R685   110   80-26837
ISBN 0-87395-524-2
ISBN 0-87395-525-0 (pbk.)

CONTENTS

ACKNOWLEDGMENT

I wish to express my gratitude to the Rockefeller Foundation for the award of a Humanities Fellowship during 1974-75 so that I might complete the major part of the work on this book.

PREFACE

This is a work about philosophy, tracing the peculiar incompleteness of philosophical explanation to its foundations in the nature of things. Such an activity is somewhat perverse, since its own incompleteness is made manifest and its reflections made mysterious. But this perversity is the heart of philosophy. As I will show, philosophy is essentially and fundamentally mysterious. It does not, cannot, solve problems or prove claims. There is something mysterious in every philosophical explanation — and by extension, something mysterious in every explanation in virtue of the comprehensiveness of philosophic understanding. Yet the principle of philosophical mystery is neither sceptical nor irrational, but expresses something fundamental about the nature of rationality. Indeed, I propose that what makes philosophy mysterious is what makes reason efficacious.

This is my major thesis. Mystery is inherent in both the nature of things and the nature of rationality. I will sustain this thesis by a review of some of the central issues of philosophy to elucidate their mysterious qualities. More important, however, I will develop in detail explanation of mystery and trace some of its important ramifications. My claim is that mystery represents a fundamental feature of rational understanding which every systematic philosophical theory must accommodate. It is manifest in all the greater works of philosophy throughout the history of philosophy and in the most powerful and effective theories in the physical and social sciences. I will offer a theory explanatory of mystery in terms of what is indeterminate in the nature of things and of

1

what is incomplete in any rational understanding. I will argue that an ordinal metaphysics, with its associated theory of query, provides an account of mystery that no other theory can provide.[1] But the case for mystery rests on the testimony of more than 2000 years of philosophy and is supported by every branch of knowledge. The particular strength of the ordinal theory is to make indeterminateness complementary with determinateness and mystery complementary with understanding, thereby avoiding completely the possibility of a destructive scepticism.

Many of the mysteries I will consider have been discussed by other philosophers, especially Wittgenstein in the final passages of the *Tractatus*, Heidegger in his later work, and John Wisdom in several well-known articles.[2] All are far more sceptical about metaphysical philosophy than I, and trace the character of mystery to language and thought more than to the nature of things. In this respect, my analysis is a sustained effort to ground the character of philosophical mystery in a metaphysical theory that avoids the inadequacies of linguistic scepticism.

The general issues implicated in philosophical mystery are set forth below in the Introduction and developed in terms of the concept of Being in Chapter I. A modest examination of the mysteries in several fields of philosophy is presented in Chapter II. Attempts to resolve the mysteries of philosophy and the world in terms of God are examined in Chapter III. These chapters establish the pervasiveness and significance of mystery, but not its nature or origins, which require an ordinal theory with its related theory of query. The theory of orders and its implications for the understanding of mystery are set forth in detail in Chapters IV and V. Finally, implications of the theory of mystery for the general predicament in which we find ourselves, sentient beings seeking to understand our conditions, control our destinies, and enrich our surroundings, are considered briefly in Chapter VI. The reader who is convinced by the earlier arguments that philosophy — along with all understanding — is mysterious may find it profitable to turn to the detailed theory of mystery directly in Chapter IV.

While the theory presented here is a theory of philosophic

mystery, it has fundamental implications for all branches of knowledge, including the physical and social sciences. That science, along with philosophy and the arts, is mysterious in its own ways, and confronts a plenitude of additional mysteries when it moves from the laboratory to the arena of life, negates unwonted optimism and unbridled faith in technological progress. But the theory of mystery is not hostile to the immense powers of the natural sciences, since they represent perhaps the most sustained programmatic effort we have undertaken to bring mysteries under control — in this case by transformation and despersal. Nevertheless, reason in the shadow of pervasive mysteries is something more than — though not other than — science; for science is but one of the major forms of reason, dependent on one of the major forms of mystery.

In short, I speak against a simplistic view of the world and of experience based on a simplistic and narrow conception of understanding and rationality. Mystery calls not for veneration and awe, but for a full and complex activity of mind, broaching all established conditions in its pursuit of answers. But the process is infinite, the mysteries unending, our surroundings inexhaustible. Reason is fulfilled as completely in mysteries which persevere throughout our efforts to resolve them as in mysteries which are resolved and dissipated, passing into new questions to which we must find new answers, in an unterminating process of rational interrogation.

INTRODUCTION

General Remarks

Is it a deficiency that philosophy makes no progress, continually finding new beginnings? Is it a scandal that philosophy is blind, continually moving but in no definite direction?

A suggestive notion is that there are philosophical problems — therefore philosophical solutions. Yet the solutions remain elusive. Perhaps philosophical problems have no solutions. If so, they are no problems. The problem is to find a real solution to the equation, $x^2 + 25 = 0$. There is no such solution and no such problem. Who shaves all men but those who shave themselves? There is no such barber and the question is spurious. A second-level problem may be associated with every putative problem: whether that problem is genuine. The verifiability principle offers a criterion for such second-level judgments; but it is too strong, excluding many genuine problems with genuine solutions. Yet there certainly are merely putative problems. "How many angels can dance on the head of a pin?" "How many undetectable gremlins inhabit the insides of my watch?" "How may induction be transformed into deduction?" There are philosophical questions which have no satisfactory answers nor methods for eliciting them. We are tempted to say that such "questions" are spurious. "A problem is genuine only if it admits of a solution *in principle*." The italicized words have never been satisfactorily explicated.

Nor should we expect them to be. For the question of what

constitutes a genuine problem may not be a genuine problem. The central thesis of my argument is that most—if not all—important philosophical "problems" are not problems but *mysteries*. They admit either of simple solutions which are not quite acceptable or of exceedingly complex solutions which perpetuate difficulties. Philosophical controversies continue to haunt us as if the greatest of philosophers could make no headway against their complexities; or instead, as if mysteries remain despite the plausibility of proposed resolutions.

An obvious approach to philosophical mysteries is in terms of the nature of problems and their solutions. Such a strategy is vitiated by the possibility that the second-order issue is also a mystery. With what issues should philosophy be concerned? If that were known (or even knowable), philosophy would be far simpler than it is, and far less mysterious.

We must therefore take a different approach. Instead of determining the nature of genuine problems with genuine solutions, I will approach the subject in terms of mystery. What remains mysterious even where philosophical understanding has been gained? What residuum prevails after philosophical analysis and judgment? Why is there no philosophical progress? I will suggest answers to these questions. Nevertheless, although there are answers, they are mysterious; for philosophy is one of the greatest mysteries. The reason looks to the heart of things, the pervasive character of what philosophy seeks to comprehend.

What is a mystery? Is it something that cannot be explained? Miracles are mysterious, yet they have explanations in terms of a divine will. Is a chance event a mystery? It is quintessentially inexplicable. Yet there is nothing mysterious about sheer arbitrariness. What has no explanation cannot be understood; but it is not in itself a mystery.

Many different kinds of things have been called mysterious, and we are free to call mysterious what we please: what we do not understand as yet, what we will never understand, what cannot be understood. The mysteries I am concerned with are none of these, though they resemble the third. We must distinguish the notion of a mystery located at the absolute limits of rationality and intelligibility from mysteries which express the limits but also the achievements of reason. On one view, mystery is located at the limits of determinateness, an attribute of indeterminateness. On the view of mystery I shall defend, determinateness and indeterminateness are complementary notions, functionally related, and mystery is therefore complementary with understanding, the two together comprising rationality. In this sense, every explanation is grounded in a mystery that requires further explanation *ad infinitum*. Nevertheless, the presence of such mystery is not a defect in reason, but a function of its powers and achievements.

A stone falls down a hill. It rains. Are these mysteries? They are events. If located in a causal or telic order, they are intelligible. If not, they may be unintelligible. Intelligible or not, understood or not, they are equally mysterious. There is indeterminateness as well as determinateness in every event, every condition, and their complementarity is the source of mystery. Every explanation testifies to mysteries and engenders further mysteries. Even if all events belong to a causal order of succession, mystery remains. How can *all* events in a complex world be coordinated within one overarching system? Why is there this rather than some other causal order? The world is a mystery.

Why is there anything at all? This is a very strange question. It is a mystery because every answer is deficient — including explanations of why it is no question. We are haunted by the question even while we reject it. The intelligibility of things makes their totality mysterious.

Why is there anything at all? One possibility is that the question is meaningless. We cannot refer without qualification to everything, anything, the universe. We cannot quantify without restriction over all beings, only over members of a given domain. "Everything" is no subject of which we may predicate properties. We may predicate only of "everything of a certain kind."

Some of the greatest philosophers have proposed an ultimate explanation in terms of God — the final limit of intelligibility. God is then the supreme mystery. He serves as a final principle of

6

explanation by absorbing all mysteries into himself. Why is there something rather than nothing? Because of God. Why is there God? Because of his nature. Every answer affirms the mystery.

We may be trying to explain what cannot be explained. If so, then it is mysterious that there is no explanation. The claim that there is an explanation from the standpoint of an infinite intellect, but that human finitude is limited, hardens the mystery. It obscures the most fascinating aspect of philosophical mysteries — that we can advance against them.

To define precisely what is mysterious in philosophy is to dissipate the mystery and to transform it into a surd. There may be arbitrariness and irrationality, and the world may be full of surds. But reason will find no mysteries there since it is forbidden to enter. Mystery is a function of rationality and intelligibility: it is most forceful when we have explanations, for they are always incomplete. We may not range in thought over the entire universe. What then *is* the universe? What then is *nature*? If we can ask the question, it has no answer. If we cannot ask it, the world is a mystery despite our knowledge of the laws of nature.

Affirming the presence of mystery is not irrationality. To the contrary, by bringing into the light the ways in which philosophical mysteries prevail with reason, we may dispel some of the confusions which surround them.

This book is inspired by the conviction that there are not one or two fundamental mysteries and many simpler problems to which definitive answers can be found. Rather, there are many mysteries — so many that they possess no mystique; so common that we tolerate them in a spirit of wonder. The great diversity of mysteries enables us to understand the error in claiming that ultimate mysteries cannot be resolved. They cannot; but then neither can any others. Mysteries confront us at every turn. Philosophy endures because it is mysterious; and its greatest mystery is that we understand so much despite the deficiencies of every understanding.

Philosophical Argument

Closely corresponding to an emphasis on *problems* is an emphasis on *argument*, as if the aim of the philosopher were to prove rather than discover, to verify rather than invent. Sometimes philosophy is thought to provide *analysis* more than argument; more often both. Yet it is generally impossible to prove that a philosophical thesis is "correct." The opposite is the case: arguments are relevant only in terms of a given analysis.

Consider the ontological argument. It has been dissected to a point of vacuousness: existence is or is not a predicate; necessary existence is or is not distinct from mere existence; the argument is or is not circular.

The persistence of so elementary an argument suggests that it masks a mystery. Part of the mystery is that of God. Part is that of existence. But there is also the mystery of argument itself. The ontological proof is about God, existence, and the universe. Yet it speaks only to the necessary existence of a perfect being. Can we reasonably expect any argument to shed light on the deepest issues of the universe?

The question is whether any argument can do justice to what is truly complex and profound. Now many well-known philosophical arguments are not inductive; and if deductive, they cannot be definitive, since deductive arguments depend on established premises. Either first principles, unquestionably true; or else, philosophical argument can only be persuasive. Scepticism lurks nearby—but only if proof is essential, if argument is necessary.

By way of contrast, Whitehead

> conceives 'proof,' in the strict sense of that term, as a feeble second-rate procedure. When the word 'proof' has been uttered, the next notion to enter the mind is 'half-heartedness.' Unless proof has produced self-evidence and thereby rendered itself unnecessary, it has issued in a second-rate state of mind, producing action devoid of understanding. Self-evidence is the basic fact on which all greatness supports itself. But 'proof' is one of the routes by which self-evidence is often obtained.[1]

8

Given the imperative that philosophy make its case known, such a rejection of argument seems absurd. Even worse is the appeal to self-evidence. Yet an important distinction is involved. Where persuasion is at stake, argument and proof are essential, the only rational means. But they are then means of confirmation, not of discovery. What we require is understanding; proof is but an important means to understanding.

Every argument proceeds from premises. Is there knowledge without premises? If not, the premises recede to infinity. If so, then argument is in principle unnecessary. In either case, though God might avoid argument, philosophers seek arguments that are intrinsically incomplete. If there is a deeper philosophical truth, it cannot be reached by argument. Conversely, philosophical argument never touches what is most important.

On the other hand — there is always another point of view — what can reasonably compel us to adopt a philosophic position other than argument? Let us argue from premises we all accept. All such premises in philosophy are trivial. Let us argue hypothetically from presupposed premises to conclusions we may examine together. We will not agree on the results of our deliberations. Let us not argue at all, but reach consensus through mutual influence. Consensus then has no authority. Philosophical truth recedes to infinity.

It is essential to the theory of mystery that there are always different sides to every philosophical issue. There is always something to be said from another point of view. Therefore, no analysis can be definitive and final. Understanding is always incomplete and stands in a mysterious relationship to argument. There is mystery in every philosophical dispute. And it is not merely the mystery of self-contradiction — demanding on the one hand what will never do on the other. It is also the mystery that a given analysis is deficient, though it is satisfactory in most respects.

Systematic Philosophy

When philosophers speak of philosophical "problems," especially permanent and recurrent problems, they may have

9

relatively independent issues in mind. There are no solutions precisely because each problem is examined in isolation. Mystery may be engendered in the inadequacy of every separate approach, the deficiencies of every isolated resolution.

An alternative is to regard philosophy *systematically*: in terms of a cluster of concepts and principles relevant to a great range of diverse issues. If we cannot resolve any of the issues independently, perhaps we may approach them collectively. If we cannot fully transform a local diversity into an identity, so that explanation forever escapes us, perhaps we may transform a great wealth of diversities into a coherent system of relations, none attaining identity, but all satisfactorily unified within a larger perspective.

There are several senses in which philosophy can be systematic. The two relevant here are: (1) a unified network of concepts and principles in terms of which a great diversity of subject matters and issues are interconnected. Spinoza is an excellent example of such a systematic philosopher, as are Hegel and Kant. Philosophy can be systematic in the literal sense of creating a system within which diverse elements are interrelated. (2) The collective consideration of a great range and diversity of subject matters and issues, though they may not be comprehensively unified under common principles. Philosophy can be systematic in the somewhat less literal sense of range and comprehensiveness. Here the emphasis is not on consolidation and unification but on breadth and scope, on a commonality of approaches to a wealth of diverse considerations. Locke is the supreme example of a philosopher systematic in this latter sense; Aristotle may also be included.

The two senses together define a straightforward approach to the difficulties of philosophical explanation. No philosophical issue of itself, isolated from other issues, can be given a definitive resolution. In this sense there are no philosophical problems. In the same sense, there are no scientific or mathematical problems: general principles always apply to a wide range of diverse issues. But to the extent that a given philosophical system—or systematic method—brings together diverse and unrelated issues, defining satisfactory approaches to most of them, to that extent do we resolve them. Systematic philosophy gains its comprehensiveness less from argument and self-evidence than from the interrelational structure of categories and principles which coordinate diverse issues into an orderly pattern.

Philosophy no doubt gains persuasiveness from its systematic character. The greater cosmologists cast a profound light on a remarkable range of diverse issues, subject matters, and considerations. Persuasiveness here is not proof but satisfaction of diverse constraints of conviction. The greater comprehensiveness of systematic philosophy makes it less satisfactory as a form of proof as it more successfully ranges over heterogeneous concerns to provide conviction. None of the individual arguments is quite definitive; of several, some are far more secure than others. An individual argument may always be attacked; several become weaker together—no stronger than the weakest link. No system can be equally strong in all areas. Every system may be attacked at its weakest point.

If there can be no definitive argument relative to any given philosophical issue, systematically coordinating them into a a relational order—though often a magnificent achievement—provides no definitive justification. To those who demand decisiveness in argument and analysis, systematic philosophy contributes little. Those who demand breadth and comprehensiveness cannot also demand decisiveness in argument.

Even worse, there cannot be a superior philosophical system, better in all ways and respects. The weaknesses of one are offset by the strengths of another. Over the broad range of diverse philosophical concerns, one approach will have its merits, another different strengths and weaknesses. On balance, one approach may seem superior—but it will always have limitations. Moreover, the very notion of such a balance seems odd. We give all the reasons why, on balance, a given philosophical method is fruitful and perspicuous. We justify accepting it. Having made our case, we note that others are unpersuaded.

Systems of philosophy are inevitably plural—and here is their fundamental mystery. For if no particular system is superior to all

11

others, each of the greater systems is superior in some respects. Only with them all together do we have a systematic complexity faithful to our deepest intuitions and conceptions. Unfortunately, philosophical systems are logically incompatible. Their assumptions are incommensurate. They conflict in their methods and justifications. We can accept none alone. We cannot accept them all together.

We can tolerate diversity among masterpieces of art, none of which is superior to the others. We may then suppose that systems of philosophy are like works of art—beautiful, fascinating, but untrue. Metaphysics has been likened to music. Both lack direct reference to concrete elements of experience. Still, where music need only move us and awaken in us awareness of its characteristic elements, philosophy must reflect upon the nature of things. It seeks truth where art may seek fascination. Philosophy is a profound mystery relative to both art and science. It is rigorously faithful to experience and the world where art can be fantastic and irrelevant; it is pluralistic and indecisive where science progresses forcefully and compellingly. Philosophy— especially systematic philosophy—is mysterious in its plurality and its demands.

Philosophy as Art

If there are no definitive and determinate philosophical answers, there are no philosophic problems. In this respect, philosophy is more akin to art than to science. In art, there are no definitive answers—and no "problems" either. Which color, in what shape, should be employed in the upper right corner of a canvas? The question has no answer—or, alternatively, too many. Artists experiment; but the "problems" they deal with have indefinitely many answers. Plurality is intrinsic to art. And if plurality is intrinsic to philosophy also, philosophy seems an art.

Consider then the following:

> Philosophy, resembling both science and art, is both assertive and exhibitive.... [There are]... two phases of a philosophical

perspective. In one of these, a philosophy constructs; in the other, it comments on the construction. On the one hand, it brings together a number of categories and develops them by analogy and metaphor and definition; in the other, it examines alternatives, excludes supposed implications, and justifies the categorial configurations in terms that do not make use of the categories. . . . The mistake to avoid is the assumption that a philosophy has two parts, in one of which the judgments are exhibitive and in the other of which they are assertive. It is the perspective as a whole which must be regarded as a judgment-complex.[2]

Here philosophy resembles science and art, but it is neither. It is a composite of exhibitive and assertive judgment. (There are three modes of judgment here: assertive, active, exhibitive.) Not only is Spinoza's *Ethics* fascinating by virtue of its geometrical structure and central categories: it is also fascinating in its delineation of a world—the intricate relationship of first principles to the causal order, the relationship of the temporal and non-temporal, the interconnection of ideas and passions, and so forth. Not only do the great works of philosophy compel our assent in virtue of their testimony concerning the nature of things; they also define a relational order that compels assent in virtue of its structure. The axiomatic structure of the *Ethics* exhibits the principle that causation is to be assimilated to logical relations, though Spinoza never quite says this. He does say that the order and connection of ideas is the same as the order and connection of things. It follows that the order and connection of propositions in the *Ethics* is the same as the order and connection of the world—though our assent to this cannot be won through proof, but by the complex interweaving of the assertive and exhibitive elements within the work.

Philosophy is not art alone—if art at all; and not science alone—if science at all. I will later show that every judgment may be regarded in any of the modes of judgment or all of them at once. Philosophy is not the only composite of modes of judgment. It remains a mystery—unless we find for it a unique mode of judgment other than the three mentioned. I will argue in a later chapter that philosophy — at least systematic metaphysics — emphasizes a fourth mode of judgment. It is to be noted, however, that such a view by no means eliminates the mystery of philosophy. It simply places it on the same level as all the modes of judgment. The central mystery is that every great intellectual enterprise — science, ethics, art, philosophy — is at one and the same time a composite of all the modes of judgment yet serves one of them predominantly, while each mode is distinct and irreducible. How can irreducible and distinct modes of judgment be conjoined, blended, admixed, even compared? Does every such admixture generate another mode of judgment? If so, there will be an infinite number, most of which are at present unknown. If not, why are there four, not five, ten, 666? Inventiveness suggests an indefinite capacity to add; yet if the world is definite, there must be definite disciplines and forms of judgment.

I have said enough by way of introduction. I will now turn from philosophy as a subject matter to specific issues of philosophy. I will begin with the elusive mysteries of Being. I will later consider the elusive mysteries of God. In between, I will range over several of the common mysteries of philosophy. In conclusion, I will return to philosophy as a subject matter, seeking a way to understand a mystery that does not collapse into irrationality, unintelligibility, arbitrariness, and chaos.

I.

BEING

The mystery of Being is ancient and recurrent, and seems permanent. With Heidegger, we may find it a source of profundity, and go back to earliest philosophy to pursue its origins. Yet we should be hesitant in speaking of *the* mystery of Being: there may be many mysteries, related but distinct. A fundamental principle is that there are indefinitely many mysteries, related and unrelated in many ways. In this respect, Heidegger's approach to Being is misleading. He speaks of the fundamental question of metaphysics.[1] The suggestion is that a single question lies at the heart of philosophy, while of course there are many.

Obedient to the central principle of plurality, I will not address *the* mystery of Being, as if one mystery takes precedence. Instead, I will examine several mysteries which look to Being for their origin. The mystery of Being is located in many other mysteries, some of which have straightforward resolutions—except that none dissipates the mystery entirely. Philosophic mysteries reside not amidst the absence of solutions, but where solutions are plentiful, each of which ought to be decisive—except that none is.

The mystery of Being is the mystery of Non-being.

The mystery begins with Parmenides: Being and Non-being are contradictories; therefore Being cannot be admixed with any Non-being. Nevertheless, Non-being is present everywhere. The

15

mystery is two-fold: that anything other than Being can be said to be—for it also fails to be; and that there is any connection whatsoever between Being and what is. The mystery is the relationship between determinateness and indeterminateness. Heidegger asks: What about Nothing? Non-being is "the negation of the totality of what-is: that which is absolutely not."[2] For the moment, we may set aside the mysteries of totalities and absolutes. It is sufficient that Being and Non-being are contradictories—entailing that everything other than Being is self-contradictory. Becoming is and is not what is (is now)(will be). Appearances are what they are and pass for (are) what they are not. All thought and meaning are contradictory in the same sense. Values are not facts—what is the case; they are then either nothing at all (thus not values), or they both are and are not what is (the case).

The mystery of Being is that there is Non-being.

Hypothesis (a): *There is no unqualified Non-being.* There is no contradiction involved in saying *Non-being is* when we are speaking of qualified or relative Non-being. A table is a table—therefore not a chair. Corresponding to every kind of being there is non-being. There may be a contradiction between Being as the totality of things and Non-being as nothingness. But there is no mystery to the conjunction of being one kind of thing and not another. More accurately, there is not *that* mystery, but there is another.

The mystery of Being is that Non-being is not.

The mystery of Non-being is a mystery of limits. For if Non-being has no limits, it cannot be anything at all. The mystery shows itself in whatever we say about Non-being. It is required for limitation and determinateness. Yet it seems to have no limits itself.

Non-being is infinite, open-ended, uncompletable: not this, not that, not something else, *ad infinitum and inexhaustibly.* "And so on" haunts Non-being—therefore, Being as well. We can never fully grasp Non-being (or Being).

The mystery of Being is the mystery of the totality of things.

Hypothesis (b): *Being is pure positivity; Non-being is relative to consciousness.* In the world there are only positive facts. Non-

16

being belongs to appearances. It is circumscribed by expectations and apprehensions. By the negativity of consciousness,
freedom finds its place in the world.

The hypothesis is mysterious. How does consciousness prevail
amidst the seamless positivity of Being? We pass into the mysteries of freedom and mind. What is is determinate — yet there is
the freedom of alternatives. And if everything is indeterminate,
there is a greater mystery.

The mystery of Being is that it requires Non-being.

The mystery of Being is the mystery of the totality of things.

To speak of Being absolutely is to speak either of a reality apart
from all individual beings or of all such beings collectively. Now
the totality of things cannot be negated or divided. The universe
as a whole cannot change — for it will still be the universe. Being
is therefore unchanging and indivisible.

What, however, is the relationship between individual beings
and Being as a whole? The mystery of many things, diverse and
relational, is transformed into the absolute mystery of the one-
ness of the world.

The mystery of Being is the mystery of the world.

Hypothesis: *The universe cannot be regarded collectively.*

(a) The universe (or Being) is nothing but the sum of beings
individually and severally. It is therefore divided; moreover,
many of these beings change, as does their sum.

In Spinoza's cosmology, Substance is one, unchanging, eternal —
extended as well as intelligible. Substance represents the principle that there is one universe founded on God. But how can
many individual beings (finite modes) all follow from one substance without dividing it? How can God be absolutely infinite,
with an infinite number of attributes, yet be one indivisible
substance? The finite cannot be wedded to the infinite; the one
remains aloof from the many. These are some of the mysteries of
the totality of things.

That Being (or the universe) cannot be spoken of comprehensively does not eliminate its mystery. The world is no object

17

of cognition: how then do we understand one world and the relations among its several beings? Do they all inhabit one universe — or are there many universes? And can we even speak of many worlds without comprehensively relating them?

The mystery of Being is the mystery of the unity of the world.

The hypothesis is that there is no one universe: that is why Being cannot be spoken of as a totality. The formal principle that Being refers only to individual beings reflects the substantive principle that the world is not one but radically inexhaustible.[3] The mystery is not of the nature of the world, for there is no "world" to have a nature, but of many "worlds," many comprehensively interrelated spheres.

(b) *The totality of things is beyond our comprehension.* We take refuge in the mystery that knowledge is restricted to phenomenal experience while the totality of things is absolutely transphenomenal. Reason strives for completion, but in vain. Nevertheless, we seek a greater comprehensiveness than is given by phenomenal experience.

The mystery of Being is that there is experience — but not only experience.

(c) There is no unqualified reality: there are only limited and circumscribed beings. "No theory of reality in general, *überhaupt,* is possible or needed."[4] There is the reality of daily experience relative to the unreality of a dream; the reality of characters in a play relative to their pretended wealth; the reality of musical experience relative to the unreality of the score; but there is no reality *überhaupt.*

The mystery of Being is that nature is incomplete.

The world is no unified being. How then are all things together in one universe? There is no such universe. Why, then, is there anything at all?

The mystery of Being is that there is anything at all.

For there might have been nothing.

(a) The existence of the world is contingent. For we may imagine the non-existence of any existing being.

18

(b) The existence of the world is necessary. For we cannot imagine nothingness. If there were no stones and clouds, nevertheless there would be empty space. Could we imagine the non-existence of empty space? (Can we imagine the existence of empty space?) We can imagine the substitution of one being for another, but not the absence of all beings whatsoever.

(c) The existence of anything is a mystery. For it looks to the existence of something else, which looks to something else, *ad infinitum*. Or if not, it is cause of itself, and.a patent mystery. The existence of the world is the mystery from which the mystery of every being departs.

(d) The existence of the world is unintelligible. For what is "the world" except the name of all things together? And we cannot sum all beings together to comprise a universe. Does the world include God, unicorns, Hamlet's sword, the number three? If so, it is no simple collectivity. If not, where are its limits?

Is there a world? There is something. But it may be many, not one; it may be multifarious, not unified. The existence of one being may depend on the existence of another; but there may be no being which is the world whose existence requires a reason.

The mystery of Being is the mystery of the world—its nature and existence.

The mystery of Being is that there is no reason for the existence of the world.

The cosmological argument builds from the premise that the world demands a reason—a first cause. Now there is some confusion as to whether *we* or *the world* requires reasons. Could the world exist without an ultimate reason, or do we require a reason to *understand* the existence of the world?

Consider the sequence of events comprising the extended universe. (Does it include the number five and Hamlet's father's ghost?) The cosmological argument asserts that although the reason for the existence of one event may lie in another, preceding event (conjoined with the laws of nature), no such reason can be complete.

19

Suppose a book on the elements of geometry to have been eternal and that others had been successively copied from it, it is evident that, although we might account for the present book by the book which was its model, we could nevertheless never, by assuming any number of books whatever, reach a perfect reason for them; for we may always wonder why such books have existed from all time; that is, why books exist at all and why they are thus written. What is true of books is also true of the different states of the world, for in spite of certain laws of change a succeeding state is in a certain way only a copy of the preceding, and to whatever anterior state you may go back you will never find there a complete reason why there is any world at all, and why this world rather than some other. And even if you imagine the world eternal, nevertheless since you posit nothing but a succession of states, and as you find a sufficient reason for them in none of them whatsoever, and as any number of them whatever does not aid you in giving a reason for them, it is evident that the reason must be sought elsewhere.[5]

The world is nothing but a succession of states, and the perfect or complete reason for the totality of states must lie outside them all.

The reasons of the world, therefore, lie hidden in something extramundane different from the chain of states or series of things, the aggregate of which constitutes the world. We must therefore pass from physical or hypothetical necessity, which determines the later states of the world by the prior, to something which is absolute or metaphysical necessity, the reason for which cannot be given.[6]

The ultimate reason for the world cannot be given, but it is necessary that there be such a reason.
The mystery of Being is the mystery of God.
Why does the world require a reason—especially a complete or perfect reason? *Hypothesis:* the world is contingent. Yet if there is a perfect and complete cause of the world, does it not make the world necessary? The contingency of the

20

world is a mystery relative to the mystery of a necessary first cause.

The mystery of Being is the mystery of what the world is.

But is it a mystery at all? Given the laws of nature and the state of the world at any time, we may determine every other state of the universe from them.

Could we know the state of the entire world at any time?

Hypothesis I: We may not do so today, but in some indefinite future. There is not the faintest shred of evidence to support this position. We may ignore the difficulties involved in knowing all the laws of nature, which are certainly infinite in number. The world is too large for us to master.

Hypothesis II: We may never know the state of the world at any time, but there is such a state to be known, Again, there is not the slightest evidence to support the hypothesis.

Hypothesis III: The world is not a unity, not one, but many. It is comprised of many interrelated strands and sequences. Why not? And if so, it is no wonder that it is a mystery—or rather, *many* mysteries.

Why is the world the way it is? According to the third hypothesis, the world is not anything, and there is no way that it is. Why is something the way it is? Because of something else, *ad infinitum.* We find the world as it is, but we can never pierce the veil surrounding it, its mysterious foundations, The reason is that there is no veil, no mysterious foundation—and that is mystery enough. The mystery is not that there is anything, but that what there is is what it is.

The mystery of Being is that Being is inexhaustible.

There are many different kinds of beings: stones, numbers, functions, clouds, dreams, the past and the future, fictions, appearances, *Hamlet,* Elsinore, Anna Karenina, soundless screams devils, and black masses. Are they all part of one world, all together in nature? There is no world that includes them all, each related to all others.

The unity of the world depends on a primary reality. All-inclusiveness can be attained only by exclusion and subordination. If all beings are equally real, there is relatedness and interconnection, but there can be no *world*.

Either there is ontological primacy, a fundamental mode of being; or else the world is not unified but inexhaustible. Either there is unification on a hierarchical basis, grounded in a fundamental reality; or else there is no unified world, only many interrelated beings. If there is Being, a totality of things, there is ontological primacy. If there is ontological parity—no being more real than any other—then being is inexhaustible.

No being is completely determinate; everything is indeterminate relative to other beings. No being is completely finished; there are always further adventures. No being is prior to all others; there is no being which does not presuppose other beings. Being is always dependent, incomplete, partial, indeterminate, limited, indefinite, relational, and open.

The mystery of Being is the mystery of indeterminateness.

The mystery of Being is the nature of the universe.

"How does it stand with Being?"

(a) Being is nothing, a vapor, a misuse of language. If so, then the unity and totality of beings is a mystery.

(b) Being is the totality of things, the guiding rule, the essence among beings. If so, there may be no totality, no common essence or rule. The mystery is whether there is a unity to the world.

(c) If there is no unity to the world, only many beings, each related to many others, and if there is no universal mode of relatedness, then Being is both incomplete and inexhaustible. What then is the world? There is no world. What then is common to all beings? Nothing:—or only that they are beings, related to and influencing other beings. Yet Being is not an essence.

The mystery of Being is that Being is not.

The mystery of Being is implicated in many other mysteries. It is time to consider some of them. The final mystery is the nature

22

of things—for although there are many beings with different natures, they comprise no world.

What could be a greater mystery, though we might fully understand why the world is no being?

II.

SOME PHILOSOPHIC MYSTERIES

M ystery pervades philosophy. Every branch, every field, of philosophy manifests its mysteries, difficulties that cannot be resolved although, with the passage of time, we come to understand more and more about them. Many of the branches of philosophy are based on characteristic mysteries. Many of the other branches of knowledge are based on philosophic mysteries, but in terms that postpone, even dismiss, their mysteriousness. Many philosophic mysteries have been prominent at certain times, neglected at other times. Some have been relatively prominent throughout the history of philosophy. Such features as prominence and importance are functions of circumstance and fashion, not of the fundamental characteristics of the mysteries themselves, which have an enduring, resistant, and recurrent nature even in their periods of recession.

Mystery pervades philosophy. But it thereby is relevant to every branch of knowledge, if only at its recesses or periphery. Philosophy is relevant, if only marginally, to every other branch of knowledge to the extent that the concepts and interrelations, the methods and presuppositions, of every field come under philosophical scrutiny. The mysteries that pervade philosophy are relevant, if suspended, within every field of knowledge.

In this chapter, I will briefly consider some of the better-known mysteries of philosophy, over a broad range of fields and subfields. In every case, I will suggest, mystery is a consequence of the multiple character and incompatible determinations of the identities of particular beings and kinds of beings. Equivalently,

24

it is a consequence of the complementary interrelationship of what is determinate and what is indeterminate in every character and condition. There are fundamental conceptual tensions inherent in our understanding of things, tensions which are transformed but never resolved through time and further inquiry. The reason lies in the nature of things, their indeterminateness and determinateness. Mystery is a function of plurality and multiplicity in beings, with attendant indeterminateness as well as determinateness. This will be manifested in this chapter by example and in particular cases. The general theory will be developed in Chapters IV and V.

Time and Becoming.

A classical mystery is the mystery of becoming—which passes into the mystery of time. Parmenides' view is the extreme: Being is one, unchanging, and indivisible. Change is made a total mystery, thereby dissipating the many deeper mysteries of time. The cosmological impulse always leads to the same end, transforming an indefinite multiplicity of mysteries into one supreme mystery of the universe.

> God is the ultimate limitation, and His existence is the ultimate irrationality. For no reason can be given for just that limitation which it stands in His nature to impose. God is not concrete, but He is the ground for concrete actuality. No reason can be given for the nature of God, because that nature is the ground of rationality.[1]

The most famous and persistent mysteries of becoming are found in Zeno's paradoxes. The mathematical features of the paradoxes have been largely laid to rest. To the extent that the *Race Course* and *Achilles and the Tortoise* depend on assumptions involving the unintelligibility of infinite sequences, we can safely consider them resolved. There is no difficulty in the principle that an infinite number of regions is contained in every region. Infinite divisibility can be defined recursively, so that another division can always be performed.

By way of contrast, however, we may consider Whitehead's statement of the paradox.

> Consider, for example, an act of becoming during one second. The act is divisible into two acts, one during the earlier half of the second, the other during the later half of the second. Thus that which becomes during the whole second presupposes that which becomes during the first half-second. Analogously, that which becomes during the first half-second, and so on indefinitely. Thus if we consider the process of becoming up to the beginning of the second in question, and ask what then becomes, no answer can be given. For, whatever creatue we indicate presupposes an earlier creature which became after the beginning of the second and antecedently to the earlier creature. Therefore there is nothing which becomes, so as to effect a transition into the second in question.[2]

Whitehead's argument is that every event must have a predecessor and a successor. But the event in which Achilles passes the tortoise can have no predecessor if each of the infinite steps comprises an event.

The point here is that our understanding of time (and becoming) is effectively divided. Change must be understood in terms of two conditions: an infinitely divisible extensive continuum and a succession of events comprising passage; but the two are incompatible. Though *time* may be infinitely divisible, *events* are not. If an infinite sequence of events cannot have passed: or if every event has both a predecessor and a successor, then events are not infinitely divisible. The relation between the temporal continuum and the sequence of events which comprises transition is an important mystery. It is not necessary to suppose that there is but one fundamental sequence of events comprising the world. It is sufficient that events be perceived as containing passage or time intrinsically, while the continuum represents time at best extrinsically in terms of relations among events. If time belongs to events intrinsically, it is ultimate and mysterious along with all ultimates. If time is an extrinsic relation among events, it vanishes into what Bergson calls "spatialization."

We may note here McTaggart's argument that time is unreal.[3] McTaggart makes explicit two distinct relations in time: the transition from past to future and the continuum of earlier to later. The earlier-later continuum is infinitely divisible. But it lacks time in two senses: it is intrinsically symmetric; it also contains no intrinsic principle of transition. In itself, the earlier-later sequence gives us no understanding of change. However, according to McTaggart, the past-present-future sequence is self-contradictory, since it assigns three incompatible determinations to the same event.

McTaggart's argument that the past-present-future sequence is self-contradictory and unintelligible ignores the earlier-later sequence. We may wonder what function it plays relative to time. The answer betrays his error: he introduces *two* sequences to represent time, yet criticizes *one* of them as inadequate. Neither the past-present-future sequence nor the earlier-later sequence alone can provide a basis for change. It is the inter-relationship of the two sequences — the one against the other — that gives us transition. In addition, his argument that there is a contradiction in the past-present-future sequence rests on the principle that events are what they are regardless of their temporal location. McTaggart assumes in effect that time is irrelevant to events — therefore unreal. He transforms the past-present-sequence into a version of the earlier-later sequence, and then argues that we cannot generate time from the interplay of two nontemporal sequences. Thus, his argument may be criticized for its self-contradictory assumptions. If events are in time, then time belongs to events intrinsically, and they vary with temporal location. McTaggart himself notes that events change at least in the respect that they continually become more past. But if they can change in one respect, they may change in others. A death is a death, but may cease to be mourned. A murder may become an assassination; a rebellion may become an act of freedom. The end of one process may initiate another. McTaggart's past-

27

present-future sequence is not in fact a temporal sequence at all, for the future is made just as determinate as the past.[4]

Nevertheless, McTaggart does capture one of the central mysteries of time — that at least two modes of relation are required to express time. He argues that the relationship between the two sequences — past-present-future and earlier-later — is either regressive or unintelligible. There are two sequences which cannot be made one. Now relatedness is a profound mystery: how something can be both identical with itself and related to, dependent on, something else. Relation implies dependence; identity implies self-actualization. The two appear to be contradictory. Time bears the mystery of relatedness within itself: whether it is unique and intrinsic or relational and dependent. Moreover, the presence of this mystery in the past-present-future sequence suggests that time is ultimate — which is another mystery. Indeed, ultimacy is a profound mystery, for it precludes essential forms of explanation and understanding.

It seems possible at this point to formulate an important principle of philosophical mystery. We wish to understand change and becoming: an explanation is proposed in terms of what does not change. The mystery is apparent. If change is analyzed in terms of something that changes, change has not been explained. If change is analyzed in terms of what does not change, change has been "explained away." If change is ultimate, it is a mystery. If change is explained away in terms of unchanging beings, it is equally mysterious, since change is not changelessness. If change is explained in terms of events which do not change, continuity is a mystery. If continuity is accepted, events are a mystery. The mystery is that what is to be understood (A) is explained in terms of something else (B), and A *is not* B. A tension is established between change and eternity, time and everlastingness, which cannot be entirely resolved; yet it cannot simply be accepted. There is a conflict between opposing principles, both relevant to the character of what is to be understood. Alternatively, there is an inseparable opposition of determinateness and indeterminateness in every being, every understanding.

Does a rational basis for what is temporal demand eternity, if

28

only in terms of natural laws? The difficulty is that eternity is self-sufficient. If so, it cannot be an explanation of events. If not, it depends on transition and events, and cannot be eternal.

Does time involve a beginning? Kant argues that without a beginning there would have passed an infinite succession of events, which is impossible. Yet he also argues that the world could not have had a beginning, since there would have been before an "empty time," and no beginning could have emerged from it. The mystery is clear: if the world had a beginning, nothing could have preceded it—yet it is reasonable to ask what did. If the world had no beginning, then infinite time has already passed, and time itself is a mystery.

If the beginning of the world is a mystery, the end is more so. If nothing can come from nothing, neither can everything pass away. The mystery is not that the world is everlasting, but that it might have an end. Yet the claim that the world has no end defines it as an individual totality. How can an individual exist without determinate boundaries? If the world is no entity, but an aggregate of events, all of them might pass away. If any can, why may not all of them together—leaving nothing? If the world will never be completed, how can it be said to be (an individual) at all?

These are all mysteries whose answers seem elusive. Every answer is indeterminate as if based in part on arbitrary premises and inadequate grounds. Kant claims that reason unbounded by the conditions of possible experience gives rise to phantasms of unresolvable speculation. An alternative is that the indeterminateness of speculative reason is a consequence of both the nature of reason and the inexhaustibility of our surroundings. More specifically, determinateness and indeterminateness are correlative and inseparable, jointly applicable to all subject matters and in all undertakings. Mystery, here, is a function of indeterminateness; but it is equally a function of determinateness and understanding. The omnipresence of mystery is entirely compatible with understanding, analysis, and explanation. It does, however, entail a plurality of forms of understanding and explanation.

29

We may note, here, the strangeness of history, for among other mysteries it contains the mysteries of time. The physical sciences, by way of contrast, are far less temporal—and where successful, seem to dissipate mystery. Now history might well pursue the same goals, seeking general principles of coordination among events, limited only by the complexity of human experience. Here the primary mystery would be that of eternity. By way of contrast, history confronts all the central mysteries of time: everlastingness, the relevance of the past, the totality of events.

The mystery of history is a mystery of the past and of the world. On the one hand, the past is thought to be finished and settled—unchangeable and unchanging. Change is assigned entirely to the present. As McTaggart notes, however, a past event changes in at least one respect: it continually becomes more past. Mead argues that the past is always of a present, history the history of the present.[5] If the past varies with the present, we have extreme relativism. If the past is fixed, it is irrelevant to the present. In addition, if the past comprises an unchanging ground for the changing present, we have the difficulties of everlastingness.

History also confronts the mystery of the completeness of the world. Does history comprise all events together, unified in a single sequence? If so, then the totality of events comprises a single system falling under the jurisdiction of historical judgment. But if there is no world system, the task of history is not to recapture and portray the system of the world through time, but to attain a judgment variable relative to different presents. The compresence of historical with scientific explanation is a profound mystery, since either all explanations are ultimately historical, or history should ultimately be transformed into a science based on natural law. A plurality of irreconcilable modes of explanation applicable to the same subject matter is always a central mystery.

What makes history unique is its continual concern with the poles of its mysteries. Science translates its corresponding concern into a search for eternal laws and structural relations, accepting the pole of everlastingness. History is continually torn between a settled past to be recaptured and a past relative to and varying with the present. If the past is settled, it can bear no intrinsic relation to a changing present. If the past varies, how is it different from the present and the future?

If we could travel into our past, how would we find it? If we could travel to a past we were not in, if only as a witness, we would have changed it that much. The past would be transformed into a future in terms of realizable possibilities. The mystery remains: *as* a past, it must not be changeable; yet the past changes in virtue of the present to which it bears relations. History comprises a unified system of all events in time; yet not all beings are unifiable into a single system.

The mysteries of time emerge from a tension between unchanging being and becoming. There are three possibilities: (a) unchanging being is primary; becoming is derivative; (b) becoming is primary; unchanging being is derivative; (c) being and becoming are complementary, and there is no unchanging being and no primary reality. In alternative (a), time and change are effectively explained away. The mystery of eternity becomes ultimate. Alternative (b) confronts the mystery of time directly: if becoming is ultimate, so is transition. There can be no explanation of becoming, no comprehensive explanation of why there are changing individuals. In addition, there is the difficulty that unchanging being, if derivative from becoming, has no foundation. Alternative (c) affirms the joint mystery of being and becoming. Mathematical truth becomes a mystery. In addition, there is the question of how being and becoming can be of equal ontological status. Finally, there is the question of how we may explain the advent of novel beings and becomings—which in the end involves unresolvable mysteries.

Alternative (b) suggests a cosmic analogy. The universe is a tree whose trunk is the system of spatiotemporal events. All modes of being other than that of events may be regarded as branches, twigs, or leaves. But the trunk is central. The model is plausible from a historical point of view; in the remote past there were only physical events, no fictions, works of art, appearances, dreams, purposes, values, and so forth. Nevertheless, if there

31

were events, there were magnitudes and relevant relations. There were also natural laws. The analogy is only superficially plausible; and it renders all qualities mysterious.

Its major shortcoming is that while works of art and scientific theories historically emerge from physical events, they play effective causal roles. Our model must be modified so that each branch can return to the trunk of the tree and graft itself there, even grow roots and sink into the ground. Now we may think of the universe historically in terms of the emergence of novel and non-physical forms of being. The world is temporal only in certain respects.

The analogy of a tree with branches which become trunks addresses many of the difficulties we have considered. If it is adequate to our experience, it renders the universe as a whole a mystery. Time in such a universe is of no primary significance; and we are faced with the mystery of why transitions and events seem so essential to us, given the character of our experience. One answer may be based on the fact that we are the kind of being who lives in and among events. The greatest mystery, however, may be that there is no ultimate mystery nor an ultimate reason why the world is what it is, complex as it is, since it is no world at all.

Freedom and Possibility

Freedom is very mysterious and challenges rational comprehension, as if it may be conceived only in opposition with what is intelligible. It seems to be found only in the interstices of an orderly world—suggesting that it is negation and disorder. It contrasts with regularity and lawfulness: a rational man, therefore, cannot maintain its rationality. Yet without freedom, there can be neither moral responsibility nor purpose and choice.

The issues of freedom take many forms, some of which have little to do with causal determinism, and many of which are of less than cosmic scope. The most pressing difficulties fall in the areas of values and moral responsibility. There are the contrast between human will and the will and knowledge of God; the contrast between liberty and social order, which is relevant to moral responsibility; and the difficulties inherent in artistic creativity, which may be traced back to the general mystery of novelty in the universe.

All these issues may be coordinated under the heading of alternative possibilities. Are there alternatives within determinate situations? If there are, we may consider how choices may be made among them. If there are no alternatives relative to the past, there is causal determinism. If there are no alternatives relative to other established conditions, there are other forms of determinism. Within human situations, we may look to significant alternatives and conditions which establish grounds for effective action rather than to a liberty which is merely the absence of constraints and conditions. Finally, individuality relative to social conditions may be interpreted in terms of possibilities remaining within such conditions for individual choice and appropriation.

The thesis of causal determinism is that all events and all their characteristics, traits, properties, and constituents are completely determined by past conditions. Yet past events alone do not determine events. At the least, natural laws are required. In addition, the qualities and activities of an event contribute to it, as do theories, fictional characters, and human expectations where relevant. Determinism is therefore implausible interpreted as the position that the past alone is determinative of subsequent events, and must be interpreted as the position that the past together with natural laws jointly determine all events and characters. In addition, all other modes of determination — formal, purposive, cognitive, logical, etc. — are to be understood in terms of efficient causation. The two relevant premises are that every being is rationally determined and that only causal determination is legitimate. Most theories of indeterminism challenge the first premise of determinism. They should challenge the second instead.

If determinism is the position that every characteristic of every event stands in intelligible causal relations with other events and their characteristics, three interpretations of causal indeterminism

33

may be proposed: (a) Indeterminism is chance deviation, a form of arbitrariness, and an inexplicable mystery central within human experience. The deficiency of such a view is that salient and significant features of experience are relegated to arbitrariness and caprice. (b) Indeterminism is a form of self-causation. Yet it is by no means clear that self-causation can be intelligibly conceived without collapsing into alternative (a). Without inexplicable departures, self-causation is but a form of causation. The coexistence of causal determination and self-determination, movement and agency, is a fundamental mystery where the two interact, since their interaction belongs to neither alone. Therefore, (c) indeterminism may be equated not with determinism or with a special mode of determination, but with a multiplicity of modes of determination. The second premise of determinism is rejected—that only causal determination is legitimate.

In Aristotle's words, "Spontaneity and chance are causes of effects which, though they might result from intelligence or nature, have in fact been caused by something incidentally."[6] One explanation is that:

> to occur 'by chance' means, not that there is no reason for the accident, but that factors, themselves determined by their own specific causes, do impinge on other processes, and alter and perhaps even destroy them, without being an essential part of those other processes, without belonging to their destinctive nature.[7]

While all processes are rational and caused, several processes may intersect in ways which belong to none of them alone. Aristotle rejects the possibility that distinct processes might always conjoin into a single process with an overarching end.

I have suggested an inexhaustible plurality of beings and modes of being, each with a distinctive character, which do not all comprise an overarching order. There is no world order, no world process. If each process possesses a mode of natural necessity, determinism entails that there is a supreme necessity to the world order, pluralism that there is no world order, no total necessity, though each process may have necessary characters. Determinism presupposes a cosmic necessity relevant to all events and processes, a necessity intelligible only on the ground that the universe comprises a single system.

Coincidence is no violation of necessity where every process is understood to have its particular determinations. There may be necessary connections and deterministic relations within every individual process. Nevertheless, the interaction of distinct processes produces "incidental causes." Alternatives are engendered where no inclusive process establishes an inclusive mode of necessity. We have here no spontaneous deviations, no arbitrary departures, but we nevertheless have complex events which cannot be given a complete explanation relative to any coherent individual standpoint, including their component processes and standpoints.

The principle that there are spontaneous deviations is a weakening of rationality and necessity. The principle of self-causation collapses into arbitrary deviation. By way of contrast, the principle of coincidence is compatible with necessity in every individual process. There is no sacrifice of intelligibility, since there is no denial of rationality in any process. What is denied is that every collection of intersecting processes comprises an overarching process and, in the extreme, that all events and processes together comprise a system of the world. The mystery here is that there is no "world."

The principle of coincidence can be applied to an understanding of human freedom and choice. In all human situations, it may be argued, there is a range of alternatives. No given conditions can make but one outcome necessary. A man falling out a window must fall, but he may scream and wave his arms. An injection will put a man to sleep, but quickly or slowly, with or without a struggle. There is no event which is compulsive in all respects; there are always alternatives in some respects. Borrowing from more traditional language, we may say that, whatever the actualities of any state of affairs, there are possibilities compatible with those actualities.

Possibilities here represent alternatives relative to a given state of affairs. Actualities are what is settled and compulsive within that state of affairs. In this respect, possibilities represent one of the modes of indeterminateness relevant to events and their characteristics, actualities one of the modes of determinateness. Possibilities and actualities are complementarily and categorically related, expressing one form of the complementary relationship of determinateness and indeterminateness.

We have noted the source of alternative possibilities. Within a system, though all relations among its constituent members may be determinate and necessary, nevertheless, insofar as there are other systems which interact with it, alternative possibilities are engendered. Moreover, possibilities are produced not only through the interaction of distinct and hitherto unrelated systems, but through the interaction of the members of a given system and their different constituents. The members of a given system may be themselves determinately related within that system; but each is itself a system with members, and its subaltern constituents may be related to the subaltern constituents of other members in a variety of ways, many of which are indeterminate relative to the overarching system. The subaltern constituents of one subsystem may interact with the subaltern constituents of another, engendering novel possibilities. Possibilities are the outcome of plural systems and subsystems in complex interrelations, a consequence of multiple modes of determination.

We may therefore define *determinism* as the principle that only actualities prevail; and we may define *multidetermination* as the principle that there are possibilities as well as actualities. The detailed definitions of actuality and possibility will be given in Chapters IV and V, along with other details of the theory of mystery. Informally speaking, actualities are settled and determinate, in that they comprise no alternatives jointly relevant within a system; possibilities are such alternatives: correlative possibilities are always relevant together. Causal determinism must assume that the entire world comprises one system; that every system is a single-valued constituent within the world order; therefore, that there is but one mode of necessity relative to this world order and that the world contains only actualities. If pluralism is correct, there is no world order, and there are possibilities located within every system.

If every sphere contains alternative possibilities, there is room for choice and freedom—though it is necessary to understand how a choice among alternatives can be more than an arbitrary selection. From what, though, do novel possibilities arise? Given the actualities of the inorganic world ten million years ago, possibilities prevailed of novel interactions. But there prevailed no possibility of the assassination of Lincoln. Until he became President, there could prevail no possibility of the assassination of President Lincoln. After he was assassinated, no further possibility prevailed that he would be reelected. Not only do novel events emerge from novel possibilities in accordance with natural laws: novel possibilities emerge also from the conjunction of actualities and possibilities; and so do novel natural laws. Until the development of sentient organisms there prevailed no possibility that organisms might conform to Fechner's law. The law was neither actually resident in conditions with conforming instances, nor were there actual individuals for which the law was a possibility. Only eternity can provide a home for such a law.

The theory of possibility thus rests on a fundamental mystery. It is not the unresolvable and opaque mystery of eternity or arbitrary deviation, but the mystery that there is no supreme order defining a supreme mode of necessity for all things.

I am proposing the thesis that there are indefinitely diverse systems comprising complex spheres of overlapping scope, but there is no supreme overarching system. Nature is not a system; there is no world order encompassing all other systems. Nevertheless, every sphere intersects with many other spheres in complex and manifold ways. It follows that there are possibilities as well as actualities constitutive of every system. Another way of formulating this condition is that every system is multiply determined.

Every event is multiply determined by past events, natural laws, formal relations, social relations, and so forth. A human event—for example, the invention of the theory of relativity— resides amidst a wealth of different, though related, modes of determination: Einstein's experiences, the history of science, the available evidence, the known laws of physics, the aims of science, mathematical development, Einstein's personal ambitions, his concern for truth, his personal and social relationships, the conditions in Germany at the time, and so forth. On a different scale, we may classify an event of discovery or invention in terms of history, sociology, psychology, psychoanalysis, science, and formal logic. Are these all subaltern sciences of a master science? The question is identical with whether there is an ideal biography to be written of a human individual. Pluralism entails that there is no such biography, but many biographies from many different points of view.

The principle of multiple determination is not one of *indeterminism*, but *over*determination. Nevertheless, multiple modes of determination may engender degrees of freedom in their coincidence. The principle does not suggest that where multiple systems intersect a gap is introduced into which alternatives may enter. That would revert to the arbitrariness of spontaneous deviation. The coincidence of distinct systems does not produce arbitrary events. The outcome of coincidence may not be necessary relative to the intersecting systems separately, but may be necessary relative to a system of which they are both constituents. However, they may not together comprise one system. Nevertheless, in a changing universe, systems uncoordinated in the past may be coordinated later — as a world government may bring about the consolidation of political and economic measures over the entire planet, though such coordination may have been absent in the past. The intersection of diverse systems, inclusive and overlapping, with diverse modes of determination, engenders alternatives, possibilities, in some cases choices and freedom.

Kant's thesis that causal determination is prevalent in the phenomenal world while moral principles are of absolute worth in the realm of action foreshadows the thesis of multiple determination. Yet we must abandon his limited conception of a duality in determination and his subordination of one mode to the constraints of another. If there is multiple determination, none takes absolute precedence. If there is precedence, it belongs to an overarching system. Kant does not consider the prospect that where morality and prudence clash, a novel order of judgment may be engendered, mating ideals with practical considerations. Yet politics may be conceived as the practical activity necessary to the scale of modern technology and world populations. Nevertheless, the diverse but jointly relevant systems of morality, prudence, and politics coexist, and none takes absolute precedence over the others.

As Kant shows, the difference between mere coincidence and a free but rational choice cannot reside in multiplicity of determination alone. The principle of multiple determination is a principle of novelty; of itself it is no freedom. We might say that in the absence of possibilities, there can be no freedom—except that there are possibilities in all spheres. We may say instead that what is actual admits of no freedom, that freedom is relevant only to possibilities. Nevertheless, established possibilities are not always chosen among.

Kant's insight is that freedom is a mode of necessity which defines alternatives relative to antecedent modes of determination. Though we may deny the strict necessity of moral obligations, and defend the openness of final causation, nevertheless human freedom depends on rational methods of appropriation and direction. Possibilities engendered through plural spheres of determination establish one of the conditions for choice; but to choose among alternatives is not to select one arbitrarily. A choice is grounded in its own terms of necessity. Kant argues that we may substitute for causal necessity another rational mode of determination—that of duty. But unless the choice is rational— that is, with its own modes of determination—it is no choice at all. However, contrary to Kant's view, modes of determination are not fixed relative to human capacities of experience and thought, but emerge from changing conditions.

I have taken an approach to freedom founded on a plurality of systems and modes of determination, There is no ultimate principle of deviation, but a ground in every sphere of constituent actualities and possibilities that can produce further possibilities and actualities. There is no realm of possibilities nor a complete world order relative to which both actualities and possibilities

39

are completely determinate. This theory is grounded in the principle that all spheres are indeterminate as well as determinate in some respects. The mystery of possibilities is a manifestation of the complementary interrelationship of determinateness and indeterminateness as expressed in the categories of actuality and possibility. The complementarity of determinateness and indeterminateness entails that explanation is always possible, in relation to every subject matter, but that it is always deficient in some respects. An ultimate, unresolvable mystery is transformed into a mystery indefinitely open to further understanding.

Mind

Can mysteries prevail where there are no questions? Our hesitation in reply indicates that the mystery of mind is pervasive. There may be no basis for the world, but without interrogation there can be no mystery of the world. Reason is a condition of all mysteries. We have barely begun to explore these matters.

Descartes' dualism established the terms for all subsequent discussions of mind although its mystery was well known to earlier philosophers. In their hands, however, the mystery was more commonly one of eternity or God, spirit in relation to the natural world. Descartes transformed the mystery by showing that mind is mysterious apart from God. Spinoza's theory is the final convulsion of the conviction that the mysteries of God and spirit are essentially one.

Two arguments can be found in the *Meditations* to support Descartes' claim that mind and body are two substances. Both arguments display compelling mysteries. The main argument stems from the interpretation Descartes gives to the concept of substance: that which is independent and which endures through change. He defines substance not simply as independent relative to its properties and conditions (a subject of predication), but as independent of other substances. Mind and body are independent of each other, though dependent on God, for Descartes accepts the distinction between created and uncreated substance.

The argument may be attacked from several points of view.

40

First, Descartes' conception of substance is arbitrary. He assumes that there *are* substances, begging the question of whether any beings are independent. However, if all modes of being are interrelated, we are forced to give up the independence of matter. Thus, one of the important mysteries of the Cartesian position is that of a material universe in which rational beings reside. Second, the *cogito* may be criticized for showing not that minds or subjects exist, but only ideas—which is assumed. The argument is circular: I think, therefore thinking is." What *kind* of being is thinking? No cogito can provide the answer. Third, Descartes' method turns on the notion of clear and distinct ideas. Mind and body are separate substances insofar as they may be conceived clearly and distinctly apart from each other.

We come to Descartes' second argument: that mind and body are entirely different kinds of beings. Bodies are extended, causally related, divisible, and so forth. Minds are unextended, purposeful, rational, indivisible. and so forth. Mind and body comprise distinct realms of being, with no traits in common. They therefore cannot be related, and are separate substances. The mystery here is one of relation. If mind and body are separate and distinct, no relation can be found between them which does not undermine their identities. We may represent this mystery in terms of the first: how a mode of being so different from matter can emerge from it. Alternatively, we may wonder how there can be a "ghost in the machine."[8] The mystery is that there is no ghost—nor is there a machine. Nevertheless, if mind is not a ghost, what else can it be? And what is the human body, if not a machine (with or without a ghost)?

The independence of mind and body is the central difficulty of Descartes' dualism. Yet it is supported, at least in part, by historical fact. Before there were men, was there not a mindless realm of matter? Where God is identified with spirit and activity, the answer is negative. But once mind is severed from God, we may easily imagine a world of purely physical events. The mystery is then how mind could emerge from such a world and how it can coexist with physical events. We need not postulate the independence of mind—though many would grant it. It is sufficient

41

to note that mind cannot be causally related to matter where the latter is a completely self-sufficient realm of being. If matter is not mysterious at all, mind is an intransigent mystery.

The mystery of mind is therefore a mystery of matter. Matter without mind is mysterious both in its activities and in its fruits—especially that it can be the source of mind. Matter conjoined with mind is mysterious in having no distinct identity. The alternative remains of relating body and mind as different aspects of a common being. To resolve the mystery of mind is to reinterpret matter as a mode of being. Idealists have always understood this, although their conception of actuality is far too dependent on the paradigm of a knowing subject.

There is a persistent mystery in idealism that is one form of the mystery of mind: that mind, appearances, comprise a complete and self-sufficient mode of being. This is the mystery emphasized by Berkeley, and it has a permanent fascination. The continuing mystery is that on the one hand, experience comprises all events related to human beings—thereby, insofar as we reflect on nature and the world, including all things under rational conception; on the other hand, experience is not a wide enough category to represent the fullness of nature. Here experience is the mystery: conceived narrowly it is insufficient as a ground for knowledge and action; conceived broadly it competes with the entire range of natural events.

The pluralistic theory of mystery to which we will come accepts a modified version of Berkeley's principle: *to be is to be in perspective.* One feature of Berkeley's position is accepted and generalized: that being "in itself" is unsupportable. Berkeley seems to accept the intelligibility of subjects in themselves. We may instead generalize his position so that nothing is in itself; everything is in perspective. The nature of every being is a function of the different systems of relationships to which it belongs. We preserve the mystery inherent in the principle that being is always qualified. Nevertheless, we dissipate the mystery that the principle imposes on physical reality. There is no physical reality "in itself": but there is material existence among other modes of being.

The mystery of mind is more general than the mystery of consciousness. Yet the two have frequently been conjoined. Consider, then, the following:

> There is, I mean, no aboriginal stuff or quality of being, contrasted with that of which material objects are made, out of which our thoughts of them are made; but there is a function in experience which thoughts perform, and for the performance of which this quality of being is invoked.[9]

> When we describe people as exercising qualities of mind, we are not referring to occult episodes of which their overt acts and utterances are effects; we are referring to those overt acts and utterances themselves. There are, of course, differences, crucial for our inquiry, between describing an action as performed absent-mindedly and describing a physiologically similar action as done on purpose, with care or with cunning. But such differences of description do not consist in the absence or presence of an implicit reference to some shadow-action covertly prefacing the overt action. They consist, on the contrary, in the absence or presence of certain sorts of testable explanatory-cum-predictive assertions.[10]

The approaches taken here are of great importance for understanding consciousness. Yet they suffer from a grave difficulty. We are told not what consciousness *is* but what it *does*. We may be conscious of being conscious—a remarkable condition that has its own mysteries—without being aware of the functions of consciousness. A remarkable characteristic of mind is that we are sometimes aware of our thoughts independent of the functions they are performing.

The difficulty, then, is that consciousness is both mediate and immediate, functional and obtrusive. It is clearly functional: purposes and intentions mediate between the present and the future; memories mediate between the present and the past; meanings mediate between what is present and what is absent. Nevertheless, consciousness is more than mediation, for it is also obtrusive and direct. This characteristic of consciousness has been described in various ways, as *qualitative*, as a *global feeling*, as *bruteness* and *vivacity*. Each of these may be characterized as immediate only in part: the mystery is that the conjunction of mediacy and immediacy is unintelligible, perhaps even contradictory, since neither seems to be of service to the other. While the two are always interrelated, their diversity renders all understanding mysterious. Mystery is fundamentally a consequence of diversity amidst unity, a dissolution of identity into relationality and complexity. An interplay of determinateness and indeterminateness.

We come now to mind in its cognitive activities, to reason and to judgment. An important feature of the pluralism required for mystery is its commitment to a plurality of modes of judgment along with a plurality of modes of being. Judgment here is defined in terms of method and validation. A sentence is an assertive judgment when interrogative considerations of assertive validation—truth and falsity—are methodically relevant. An act seeks validation in terms of controlled consequences relative to general ideals. Construction seeks validation in forms that emphasize enduring interest and controlled achievement. Syndesis seeks the establishment of novel orders of extraordinary comprehensiveness. And there may be other modes of judgment than the four: narrative judgment in history, formal judgment in mathematics.

The plurality of modes of judgment is the immediate mystery. Before considering it, however, we may explore the complexities of plurality somewhat further. There are at least four modes of judgment, but they intersect in complex and ramified ways. In particular, no individual judgment belongs to any mode alone, though language is deceptive on this point. A claim is an assertive judgment, and belongs to that mode alone. But the utterance of words is not only a claim but an act, a created structure of words, or a contribution to our attempts to gain comprehensiveness. Any human judgment is located in all the modes at once.

The great enterprises corresponding to the modes of judgment partake of this intermixture of modalities. Science emphasizes assertive judgment, but cannot be regarded as assertive judgment alone. A scientific study is a created work with aesthetic values, though we frequently neglect them.

Publication is an act, and may be evaluated morally. Analogously, an action may be regarded as an assertion about certain normative principles in relation to circumstances. Morals may be regarded also in terms of a constructive style of life, character, and personality. Art is predominantly constructive judgment. Yet certain arts frequently utilize explicit assertions—literature and drama—while others are regarded as implicitly assertive about artistic qualities or means and ends. The relevance of assertive judgment within every work of art engenders the issues of truth in art. The relevance of active judgment to art leads to the issues of morality in art. Every work of art is the fruit of the artist's actions and is open to judgment as an act with particular consequences. Art also provides unification and comprehensiveness, bringing together diverse elements into the embrace of a single image or work. Philosophy—in particular, metaphysics—emphasizes syndetic judgment and continuities among disparate modes of being. It is assertive, if not a science, active, constructive, and comprehensive, creating new and complex spheres of judgment and understanding.

The interplay of plural modes of judgment, especially as they are interrelated in important activities, defines a great mystery. On the one hand, none of the modes of judgment is predominant—be they four or many more—and no supreme mode of judgment comprises them all. On the other hand, every mode of judgment is unintelligible in fundamental ways from the standpoint of the others. Each is mysterious as a mode of judgment with a unique mode of validation from the point of view of the others, and there is no standpoint in terms of which such a mystery can finally be resolved. Corresponding to metaphysical pluralism and the principle that there is no all-encompassing world order there is no all-encompassing mode of judgment.

There is plurality but not complete encompassment. Nevertheless, there are always new and more comprehensive works—as a philosophical theory may organize diverse spheres of experience and judgment into a systematic whole. Reason is the

45

continual interplay of judgment and validation, invention and criticism. But there is no completion available to reason. This is a supreme and pervasive mystery: that judgment is plural, the world is plural, and there is interconnectedness but not total relatedness. No being can be fully known—in any or all of the modes simultaneously. The mystery is that plural modes of judgment are always relevant to any subject matter, with no independent method for adjudicating among them. From the other side, however, the omnipresence of such mystery is a continual challenge to thought and a continual adventure for our rational capacities.

Value

The mysteries of value need little detailing. They are among the most persistent mysteries. They may be viewed in the context of other mysteries—most obviously, those of mind and freedom. In addition, there are profound mysteries implicated in the relevance of different kinds of values to the various branches of knowledge. It will be sufficient to note but a few of the mysteries of value, sketching the considerations that make them mysterious.

The first section of Part III of Hume's *Treatise* expresses the major difficulty facing theories of moral value—that moral distinctions are derived neither from reason nor matters of fact. Yet by denying that moral principles have a basis in facts, we eliminate their most natural justification. Hume's central argument is that moral maxims must influence the will and lead to action, while knowledge of facts alone cannot determine action. Deliberation must be distinguished from performance. We have here an important insight concerning normative judgment; yet it may be no more than that assertion and action are distinct modes of judgment. Were reason to determine action entirely, the latter would be a mode of assertive judgment.

Hume's argument neglects certain facts—especially those concerning the agent. Suppose it were a fact that certain events caused violent revulsion in all of us by means of sympathetic

46

response: the suffering of others unendurable. Suppose harming others caused paralysis of will in us, making our status as agents questionable. Should we not conclude that to cause suffering is evil, destructive, and self-destructive, a consequence of our human natures? Hume's own theory of a moral sense might be interpreted as factual: in addition to facts about events, we need to know facts about human responses and the development of character.

Nevertheless deliberation is not action. Let deliberation be the consideration of all relevant facts within a given situation to the end of extending control into other situations. Let ideals be regarded as general hypotheses concerning conditions of success and failure. We have a method similar to rational methods in science: general hypotheses grounded in facts and circumstances and modified by changing conditions. In such a context we might well claim that facts alone are relevant to moral deliberation.

Nevertheless, deliberation would not be action. It might not produce decision. It need not produce a firm sense of duty. Active judgment is not assertive judgment even in the extended sense which includes deliberation. The mystery is not simply the logical disparity of facts and values, but of two distinct modes of judgment. Diverse modalities of judgment and reason, where they do not produce a rational sum, produce unresolvable mysteries where they intersect, for each is unintelligible in certain respects from the standpoint of the others. Here the mystery of value is a mystery of plural modes of judgment and validation.

The mysteries of action are expressed in the mystery of moral decision: no matter what conditions and facts are taken for granted, no matter what principles are taken as ideals, no matter what our feelings and intuitions may be, there is a gap between deliberation and action. By decision I mean that judgment which culminates in action.

There is a peril in action that cannot be avoided. We seek to gain control over alternative possibilities and to establish successful resolutions. We draw upon past history and our detailed knowledge of circumstances; but none of these determines the result. In science, we say that knowledge is fallible. But in science, the goal is not control over particular events. The mystery

47

of decision is due to this difference: that in action the individual case is paramount, while general principles are instruments of control. Fallibility is but a technical difficulty in science. In active judgment it is a source of failure.

Another important consideration in action is the interrelation of narrower and wider spheres of control. We may distinguish between actions that affect few or many individuals—between *morals* in the sense of the circumscribed or private, and *politics* in the sense of large-scale or public. Moral actions may be thought of as those which involve but small numbers of men; political actions involve great numbers. A difficulty is that no clear line can be drawn in practice between the moral and the political. Far more important, actions which seem to have effects on small numbers of men may turn out to be of political magnitude while political acts often have moral implications for individuals and their associates.

Nevertheless, moral and political spheres of action, while interrelated by practical considerations and by common standards and ideals, possess distinct standards of evaluation—for example, goals of individual satisfaction as against national destiny. It is possible to view politics as the expansion of collective and wide-ranging spheres of action at the expense of individual spheres except those which are means to political power. At the extreme, we have totalitarian forms of collective society. An alternative is that of political liberalism where individual spheres of control are regarded as the sole ends of action and political measures but means for realizing individual powers. Action is the extension of control from an established sphere to a different sphere of action—if only into the future. Many of these extensions are not temporal but social—the coordination of individual ends and practices in families and communities. Now a community can take on a life of its own—and to some extent always will. Given many individual spheres of action, can we expect that a comprehensive coordination can be attained not only among individual spheres but including wider social and political orders?

This is the major issue of political action, often posed in terms of specific forms of government or the tension between morality and expediency. Now if expediency is thought of as a total lack of principle, it can be justified on no grounds whatsoever: it does not even manifest intelligence. But if defined as following principles concerning individual or national ends instead of general or human ends, it reflects the major constraint of politics: that there are diverse spheres of action and control, and there may be no ideal accommodation among them. Moreover, the institutions which wield political control have both individual citizens and groups of men as their constituents. Can all individual and group needs be accommodated in one overarching political order? It is as mistaken to expect to establish measures and policies equally satisfactory to all men as to believe that there is a world order. There is no total political order either.

It follows that politics at its best can be but a dynamic, often torturous, interplay of policies and institutions to provide large-scale coordination among individual actions. A perfect balance, a golden mean, cannot be attained among institutional and individual concerns. Such a harmonization would achieve a perfect and most comprehensive order of human action and control. Where not all individual powers can be maximized, and choices must be made among them, only time and experience can determine which measures are most satisfactory in the context of political conflicts and powers. The mystery is persistent and obtrusive: that all large-scale actions will fail for some individuals, relatively speaking. A price must be paid for all political undertakings. Morals and politics—spheres of control of narrow and larger scope—will always be diverse. Failure in some respects and for some individuals is certain in large-scale spheres of life and action. The mystery of politics is the mystery of action in a perilous and plural world lacking absolute and all pervasive values.

A related mystery is that of progress. Has there been progress? Many men will reply negatively: there is still poverty, crime, and unhappiness. Others will point to improvements in medicine and technology. Certainly there has been progress in some respects—

longevity and freedom from disease. The question is whether there could be progress in *all* respects. Those who deny progress claim that the total quality of human life has not improved. It may be said that they are insensitive to the advances of science and technology. On the other hand, optimists who believe in progress—if there are any left today—seem insensitive to contemporary problems as well as to the felt sterility of life in affluent societies.

My concern is not with whether there has been progress but whether there could be. Ideally, progress would be an improvement in all aspects of human life. This is not only unlikely: it is absurd; for in complex spheres of experience, there can be improvement only at some expense. In less ideal terms, progress is the general improvement of human life even where there is a decline in certain spheres of life and action. Could there be such progress?

I have answered this question negatively also. There could be progress even in the weaker sense only if a satisfactory adjustment could be attained among diverse individual interests—that is, if there were an ideal political order. This is impossible. There cannot be a perfect adjustment among diverse individual and collective concerns. Even were politics to attain its goal of increasing the powers of men generally, it would be at the expense of some individuals and some values. Political and social plurality entails that some authentic values will of necessity be sacrificed in order to attain others.

Progress is thus a mystery, since it is a goal we must strive for, yet can never attain. There can at best be progress in some respects—which is no progress at all from another standpoint. Nevertheless, there are important respects in which human life has been improved. The subject of progress manifests in a vital way the mystery of a plurality of values—that decisions are to be made among competing values while there is no independent basis for choosing among them nor a privileged balance of them taken all together. Moral and political actions might be as careful and rational as possible, reflecting all relevant conditions and ideals, but they would still frequently fail in some respects.

The complexities of moral values are commonly acknowledged. The difficulties of aesthetic values often engender despair. So complex are greater works of art, and so forbidding are prospects for a general understanding, that philosophy of art has at times been rejected in principle: individual works are to be understood, criticized, and interpreted, but general theories of art are indefensible. Such a conception of art manifests it to be a profound mystery. Nevertheless, mysteries are everywhere in philosophy: art may be no more mysterious despite its richness and complexity.

The mysteriousness of art is partly due to the extraordinary emphasis laid upon individual works. We are told to pay attention to the work itself and only to the work. Now to what else might we pay attention? If we consider matters of justice and the cruelty of men, are we violating *The Brothers Karamazov?* There is a double tension in aesthetic response: we must consider and emphasize the uniqueness of the work; yet we can affirm this uniqueness only by reference to other works and to experience in general.

The difficulty is that every being is unique in some respects while every work of art is similar to other works in certain ways. A given work by an artist resembles his other work—though it differs from it also. A work inhabits traditions and genres: and they are relevant to its values. Should we read a poem as if no other poems had been written or in light of them? In what sense are we involved in the uniqueness of works of art more than their similarities to other works? In this context we may note the importance of style.

Can one work be *more* unique than another? It is by no means clear that uniqueness admits of degrees. Perhaps we mean that a work is more original—though inventiveness is also difficult to quantify. Let us say instead that a work of art is to be appreciated in the specific ways in which it is original. However, every being is unique in some respects, and may be appreciated for its uniqueness.

It is sometimes said that the aesthetic attitude is to be contrasted with a practical point of view. We are to respond to a work of art uniquely, not as an instrument to an end. Now all beings and all acts have consequences—including works of art. The aesthetic attitude is mysterious in its rejection of consequences, for some are surely relevant to artistic values—the responses of the artist and audience, for example, the sensuous impact of the work.

We might say that in responding to things as instruments we emphasize their nature and kind: a being of a certain kind has certain consequences. But a work of art is unique. More accurately, it is a creation, and is to be judged by its own standards. Now originality is a very high artistic value—though not supreme: but it presents us with the mystery of how there can be unique standards applicable to novel beings. There is a profound mystery here: that a work of art may be evaluated although subject to no standards but its own.

Shall we say that artistic creativity is faithful to no norms, no standards? That would be absurd, for we evaluate works of art. Moreover, there is no total freedom of the imagination. The mind reflects its surroundings and draws its powers from its environment. The creative imagination is bound to its conditions yet creatively free—nearly a contradiction. Even worse, the alternative to submission to established conditions is arbitrary deviation, which affords no value. Creativity contains the mystery of how there can be departures that establish standards. We may postulate that artists have been geniuses, but we do no more than enshrine the mystery of their imaginations and overpower our understanding of the artistic process.

The artistic process can be understood only very little. In part, this may be due to the variety of processes involved. In further part, the artistic process manifests the mystery of novelty. A remarkable mystery is that the artistic process deeply involves the artist in his history and circumstances yet promotes novel results. We can trace an artist's work to his past and to his childhood, even to a racial unconscious. Yet it is not exhausted in any or all of these conditions. The artistic mystery is a paradigm for all our mysteries—which are indefinitely amenable to understanding yet never exhausted by it.

We again must consider the plurality of modes of judgment as a source of mystery. A detailed examination of this source will be undertaken in later chapters. The point here is that just as the disparity between facts and values reflects a duality of modes of judgment, the uniqueness and mysteriousness of art from the standpoint of facts and morality reflects a third mode of judgment. I have called this constructive judgment: that mode in which works are created and constructed, dependent on a unique mode of validation, neither on truth and falsity nor moral rightness and wrongness as such.

The mystery is that there are many modes of judgment with unique methods and modes of validation, but the modes interpenetrate: every judgment may legitimately be evaluated in terms of any modality. Thus, a work of art is at once a manifestation of the artist's experience, a creative act, and a moral affirmation. It may be evaluated descriptively, morally (in terms of its contribution to mankind), and aesthetically. If an ideal biography could be written of an artist, it would place his work simultaneously in all the relevant modes, a causal consequence of his life and experience, a moral affirmation, a contribution to society, and a contribution to art. But there is no such biography: there is disparity and incompatibility between every pair of modalities of judgment brought under joint consideration. Art has recurrently been subjected to moral and factual analysis—in every case mysteriously and incompletely. Every mode of validation is mysterious from the standpoint of other modes. Art is simply the most visible manifestation of the plurality of modes of judgment— their idiosyncracy and their interrelations. In this sense, it is remarkably mysterious.

III.

GOD

There is a sphere where mystery is gladly acknowledged. *God is the great mystery.* This principle is accepted by those for whom there is vitality in religion as well as by those for whom the universe is an enigma that reaches its completion in God. I have noted the recurrent tendency to transform all important mysteries into the final mystery of God, who absorbs all other mysteries into that of his perfect being.

The divine has served philosophers and theologians alike as the seat of all mystery. Yet we may consider a relevant principle: where all mysteries are absorbed into one supreme mystery, it becomes intransigent. A supreme mystery effectively abolishes all other mysteries, transforming science into unholiness and philosophy into theology. To make God alone mysterious—or in secular form, the existence of the world— is to deny that anything else can be equally mysterious, while that mystery is placed beyond all rational comprehension.

To say that what is mysterious lies beyond all rational comprehension is ambiguous: "*all* rational understanding" may mean *any* rational understanding: the mystery is opaque. The expression may mean instead that no rational understanding can entirely dissipate the mystery, that there is mystery in all undertakings. The first interpretation is hostile to rational pursuits; the second welcomes them. I will strengthen the compatibility between mystery and rationality: there cannot be knowledge without mystery. The mysteries of God and the divine must be located in relation to other philosophical mysteries, as religion must be

54

located among the modes of judgment. For there are mysteries that do not foster rationality, but oppose it. Yet even these mysteries lend themselves to philosophic understanding and to all the forms of rationality.

The Divine Attributes

The attributes of God are the seat of all the divine mysteries — especially if we include existence. *What* God is has always been the greater mystery conjoined with the mysteries of his relationship to man. God has been called a spider. That is not much more mysterious than the attributes commonly assigned to him. Nevertheless, though it is a ready conclusion that these attributes are misconceived, and either there is no God or one very different from our common conceptions, that is by no means the only possible conclusion. There is also the possibility that the mystery of God is intrinsic and ineradicable, and that our rational expectations are presumptuous.

There are religions which lack reference to the supernatural and religions without a sense of divine perfection — either in power, knowledge. or benevolence. I will restrict my discussion to the greatest attributes assigned to God, particularly those related to his absolute perfection. I will consider less extreme forms of religion subsequently.

(1) *Existence.* In what does a man believe who believes in the existence of God? On many interpretations, what he believes cannot be expressed, for God is absolutely unique. Not only can we not prove that God exists: we cannot even say what that existence might be like. If the nature of God is a great mystery, the existence of God must be greater. Or is it no mystery at all, for no such being can exist? Even the denial is unintelligible, since the kind of being involved remains undefined.

The existence of God, like all other existence, should be regarded as no attribute, for existence is not a predicate. A priori arguments for the existence of God err in treating his existence as an attribute. The mystery here is that the existence of God is unique, as are all his attributes. If so, then even his existence conforms to extraordinary standards.

(2) *Perfection.* Western religious traditions since Christ have assigned to God absolute perfection. But God is also assigned very human traits—patience, tenderness, love, jealousy. There is much to be said for those forms of theism which regard the divine as a first cause completely separate from the world: they avoid the need for reconciling its perfection with more conventional attributes and its infinite nature with finite events. Anthropomorphism is a persistent difficulty for all theologies, since God's perfection must be unalloyed if he is to merit unqualified worship, while his human qualities are necessary to call worship forth. Theology tends to support the absolute perfection of God at the expense of religion, while religion establishes practice in terms that undermine divine perfection. Theology and religion are in this respect opposed. The mystery is one of absolute respect: whether an ultimate commitment can be given to a God who stands in any relation to worldly events including worship. Can a God who demands respect deserve it?

Absolute perfection is opaque. Relative perfections may conflict: perfect power with perfect beauty; perfect goodness with perfect freedom. Moreover, neither goodness nor beauty seems to admit of perfection. Perfect goodness might be attainable only by a being without a will which may be no goodness at all. Relative perfection seems not to apply to all the divine attributes—if to any. And absolute perfection is opaque, an intransigent mystery.

(3) *Goodness.* Where God is thought perfect, he is thought perfectly good. And even where God is thought imperfect, he may be thought benevolent. Still, there are religions whose gods are neither perfect nor benevolent: they arouse fear and obedience more than respect and affection. It follows that goodness, like perfection, is not necessarily a trait of the divine—indeed, there may be no attribute of divinity common to all religions and gods including existence. Yet the Western God is often said to be necessarily good.

There are several mysteries of divine goodness. Neither the

absolute infinitude nor absolute perfection of God entails moral goodness, for morality may admit of neither infinite nor absolute perfection. Morality seems to have a typically human and finite function, and an infinite being is often conceived as aloof and unconcerned about moral affairs. Murder is immoral; but the death of a man seems irrelevant from a cosmic perspective.

Relevant here is the problem of evil, yet there is no such problem given merely a perfectly good God. What is required in addition is omnipotence; for a God that is both perfectly good and perfectly powerful should have created a world free from evil. The problem of evil is a problem of *perfection*. In Hume's words, "Is he willing to prevent evil, but not able? then is he impotent. Is he able, but not willing? then is he malevolent. Is he both able and willing? whence then is evil?"[1]

The typical answers are: (1) From a divine standpoint, evil is really good. This reply establishes the permanent and intransigent mystery of evil—and of goodness as well. Morality in the human and divine orders are unrelated. (2) From a cosmic standpoint, there is harmonization of opposing interests and all may be good. Yet a balance of pleasure does not cancel pain. There is the further question of whether such a harmonization is intelligible, or whether a plurality of irreconcilable interests is not closer to the truth. This is the mystery of the totality of the world. (3) All will become good in the realization of God's purpose. Yet as Ivan Karamazov asks, can a perfect world tomorrow compensate for suffering today? The primary mystery of evil is not of morality and goodness at all, but of the supreme totality of things reconciled in God's being.

(4) *Omniscience.* Where God is thought perfect, he is thought all-knowing. And this—like all attributes of God's perfection—has grave difficulties. The most obvious is analogous to the mystery of divine goodness: God's knowledge, if perfect, can bear no resemblance to knowledge as we understand it. Human knowledge is fallible and limited; God's knowledge is perfect and complete. Prediction and inference are irrelevant. In what respect, then, can God be said to know factual, contingent events? This is

a mystery of eternity. Moreover, while it is a mystery that God might have a body, it is an equal mystery that he might have a mind.

Augustine argues that God's omniscience is not incompatible with free will, for God's knowledge is of what men will freely choose: his knowledge is outside of time. Now an active and immanent being outside of time is a divine mystery. We may put it aside. The immediate difficulty is that complete knowledge of all events entails that the future is actual relative to a divine standpoint. God's omniscience is effectively antithetic to possibilities, rendering everything actual from a cosmic point of view. God's omniscience is incompatible with a genuinely open future and is a mystery of eternity and time.

(5) *The Divine Power.* Spinoza defines God as absolutely infinite substance. He concludes that the essence of God is power—absolute and infinite. Nevertheless, Spinoza's God is not omnipotent in the common sense of that term, for he lacks will. Now the concept of divine will is remarkable. The human will, we may say, is the effort involved in action and attaining a purpose. Yet to have a purpose and to attain it are one and the same for an omnipotent being. If the will is the basis of action, but to will and to act are distinct, then either God acts without willing or he wills and acts in one—and both are mysterious. For an omnipotent being, there are no possibilities, no alternatives, therefore no action or will.

The central difficulty is that all-powerfulness is not power, not action, not willing at all. Perfection abolishes the opposition on which attributes depend. God's infinite power, if he cannot choose, is equivalent to a complete lack of power. The mystery is that a God who can act and choose, who wills and decides, is all too human: not a perfect God at all, but only a being with superior will and powers.

(6) *Uniqueness.* Tillich argues that unless God is absolutely unique, he belongs to the world, and to worship him is to worship an idol. With this claim we directly confront the intransigence of God's absolute perfection. On the one hand, unless God is absolutely unique, he merits only qualified respect—that due a

58

greater power or a superior truth and goodness. No absolute commitment can be justified for such a being; only one balanced against other ideals and powers. In the respect in which God may be similar to other, natural beings, he possesses only a relative worth.

On the other hand, absolute perfection and absolute uniqueness are both unknowable and utterly mysterious. If God is absolutely unique, none of his attributes resembles human or natural qualities. In what sense, then, are his goodness and wisdom merits rather than defects? In what sense is his uniqueness a perfection rather than a defect? If God is not absolutely perfect and unique, he cannot merit absolute respect; if he is absolutely unique, he cannot merit respect at all. It follows that God cannot be given justified worship—which is either sin or a profound mystery. God must be absolutely perfect to be God (though there are religions without such a God); but he cannot be absolutely perfect and stand in any relation whatsoever to human life.

Godless Religion

Can there be religion without God? The question is mysterious. We must determine the nature of both God and religion to answer it. There have been religions without God—religions with only demons, religions with a sense of cosmic order. There have been religions for which the universe is divine—and no God other than the universe.

There are and have been religions without God; that should settle the possibility of a godless religion. Shall we also say that there might be Christianity without God—Christ an exceptional human being, his life a unique historical event? We understand the following response: "However absurd talking about God might be, it could never be quite so obviously absurd as talking of Christian faith without God. If theology is possible today only on secularistic terms, the more candid way to say this is that theology is not possible today at all."[2]

Where God is the foundation of religion, it is absurd to propose godlessness; yet to the extent that reason fails to justify belief in the divine, a godless religion is a possibility inherent in other religious practices. If we repudiate God but maintain the social and mythic elements of a religion—say Christianity—is it not still a religion, still Christianity? Not to one for whom God is the foundation; assuredly to one for whom a mysterious God is irrelevant. These differences are akin to those among religions—a matter of indifference on the one hand, where to be religious is what is most important; yet on the other hand, the difference is about what is of ultimate concern.

The issue is not simply of God in religion and of conflicts among religions, but of the relationship between religion and the other modes of judgment. Is religion a unique mode of judgment? Is it a mode of judgment at all? If it is primarily assertion, it will conflict with science; if it is primarily action, it will play a dogmatic role; if it is a form of art, it need not conflict with other art—for works of art do not conflict: but its moral role may then be unintelligible. There remains the possibility that religion is a unique mode of judgment, or that there is another way to conceive it. I will now consider this issue, beginning with a closer look at plurality in religion.

Religious Pluralism

In his *Varieties of Religious Experience,* James points out that "the word 'religion' cannot stand for any single principle or essence, but is rather a collective name."[3] The entire work is a manifestation of the principle that there are many religions and many qualities essential to religion, which admits of no single essence. Because we are plural and diverse beings, religion will take plural forms.

James's formulation of pluralism is suggestive though limited:

> Things are 'with' one another in many ways, but nothing includes everything, or dominates over everything. The word 'and' trails along after every sentence. Something always escapes. 'Ever not quite' has to be said of the best attempts made anywhere in the universe at attaining all-inclusiveness.[4]

This is a pluralism of partiality. James rejects an all-inclusive order; but the rejection is negative. It is consonant with his spirit to conclude that there may be no supreme, final being at the core of religion.

Religious pluralism confronts three issues: First, there is the conflict between ultimate commitments and a plurality of religious experiences, forms, and activities. Second, there is the relation of plural religions to plural realities. While plurality in art is a manifestation of plural creations, religious plurality seems to have no equivalent function. Third, religious plurality suggests plural relations among the various modes of judgment and a complex set of roles for religion to play. Is religion a unique mode of judgment or merely a special form of one or more of the others? I will now respond to each of the issues posed.

Religious Judgment

The question is whether religion reflects a predominant mode of judgment and, if so. whether it is unique or among the four discussed. On the surface, there is no universal and typical human function that is central to religion—not in the way assertion is an expression of *saying*, morality of *doing*, and art of *constructing*. Saying, doing, and making are pervasive human functions. By comparison, *unifying* (syndetic judgment) seems not so widespread. On the other hand, unification is pervasive within the other modes of judgment. Worship is closest to a universal function in religion, yet there are religions where worship is absent. Nevertheless, if there is no obvious function belonging to all religions, there is a nearly universal character to religion: it seems as typically a human trait to be religious as to be rational. Religion and art are more pervasive in human life and experience, through diverse cultures and ways of life, than science and even ethics in its more systematic forms.

What are the characteristic elements of religion, and do they comprise a single essence? It would appear not. The most obvious characteristics are the following—and none belongs universally to all religions:

a. The Supernatural. Many religions accept the principle of an order transcending nature. The natural order is felt mundane and confining. The alternative is a transcendent order of intrinsic vitality toward which religious experience points. Nevertheless, there are religions where only the entire natural order is felt divine.

b. Theism. The notion of extraordinary beings with extraordinary qualities plays a role in many religions. But there are pagan religions with many gods and religions with no gods whatsoever—at best world principles underlying the natural order or a conviction that the divine resides universally in the spirits of men and animals.

c. Faith. Christian religions have emphasized the opposition between science and religion, leading to an opposition between reason and faith. God's word is revealed in an extraordinary way and our response takes extraordinary forms. Yet there are religions where the will of God is manifest through human functions—books and teachings—and takes no forms opposed to reason.

d. Worship, Ritual. There are religions in which prayer is central and others in which prayer is unknown. Nearly all religions involve common rituals and forms of worship—though there are religious men for whom piety is individual and personal, lacking all ritualistic and social forms. Among the most important characteristics of religious practices are the social forms and theological principles that play a religious role. But even here there is nothing which can be considered part of all religious experience.

e. Piety. An alternative is to define a uniquely religious attitude: devotion or piety. All religions involve adjustment to the sense of the divine, but not all emphasize a particular devotional attitude, even a conformation to specified norms. James emphasizes the great variety of religious experiences, and it is difficult to see how any particular mode of experience can be definitive of religion. We might speak of ultimate concerns, but the relevance of ultimate ideals is as critical for morality as for religion.

f. Comprehensiveness. We come, then, to a different way of approaching religion, not relative to any particular traits, but inclusive of them all. The most striking feature of established religions is the comprehensive role they play in human life. A religion maintains some components of belief—often but not always in a transcendent order, often but not always relative to a supreme being or beings, usually accompanied by and demanding extraordinary attitudes, devotion, faith, and worship, and usually accompanied by social rituals and common forms of practice. In addition, most religions exercise a moral function determining certain ideals and ultimate principles. And all religions find expression in symbolic form, both within the arts and in their practices. Finally, if philosophy is presented in a religious setting, both religion and philosophy together—at least in some works— comprehensively organize many aspects of the world and experience. In other words, it is plausible to regard religion as essentially syndetic in character, providing a unified perspective upon the world and among the modes of judgment. Religion effects unification within human experience where it would otherwise be lacking given the plurality of beings and modes of judgment.

I have associated philosophy—at least, metaphysics—with syndetic judgment.[5] How are we to understand religion in this context? My answer is that metaphysics is syndetic judgment in discourse, and is unrestricted in an important way. Science is syndetic judgment relative to assertion; ethics is syndetic judgment relative to life and action; art can provide syndetic judgments in the context of and emphasizing novel creations. All the modes of judgment are potentially comprehensive, though that is only one of their potentials. In metaphysics, this comprehensive function is predominant. In religion. comprehensiveness is also predominant—but it is qualified and hypothetical.

If there are fundamental and pervasive human functions— saying, doing, making, and unifying—they may be associated with modes of judgment only insofar as there are methodic criteria of validation appropriate to them. But there are many methods that provide conviction which are not self-critical. Assertive, active, constructive, and syndetic judgment are all modes of judgment; but they become cognitive and rational only insofar as

63

they are transformed into *query*.[6] By query I mean methodic activity that is indefinitely inventive and interrogative. Science, ethics, art, and philosophy are modes of query: they are the four modes of judgment transformed into query through ongoing methodic interrogation. They are interrogative judgment for its own sake. We may add that the modes of judgment interpenetrate, and that query relative to each implicates the others. In this respect, science involves action and construction; ethics involves assertion and the construction of a style of life; and so forth.

It is plausible here to introduce here an important distinction. Query is methodic, inventive, concerned with validation, and indefinitely interrogative. Nevertheless, there can be indefinite interrogation largely within the boundaries of a single mode of judgment — *modal* query — and query which intrinsically interrelates the modes of judgment — *intermodal* query. Religion might be query emphasizing syndetic judgment except that the moral relevance of religion would be difficult to explain, as would its symbolic character and its component of belief. The alternative is that unlike metaphysics, which is intermodal but which emphasizes syndetic judgment, religion is intrinsically intermodal — but it is not a form of intermodal query, since it is limited in fundamental respects.

Religion is not a form of intermodal query, for it is not indefinitely interrogative. By query I mean not only that there is an indefinite number of questions, but that everything may be called into question. This is a consequence of the pervasiveness of every mode of judgment — that everything in human life is open to judgment in any of the modes or all of them at once. Query involves unremitting interrogation in the two senses that questions never cease and that nothing is outside interrogation. The essential feature of religion, however, is that some domain of experience is established as permanently and intransigently mysterious, in that respect outside query. Whether it be the existence of God, the holiness of certain books, the sanctity of certain rituals, even the immediate character of certain experiences, there is some domain of experience, some character of every religion, that is essential to it yet beyond question. When such

64

received truths are questioned, religion passes over into philosophy.

Religion is syndetic judgment—though not syndetic judgment alone—for it organizes and conjoins a great variety of activities and experiences within a practice and a style of life. Religion trafficks with morality, cosmology, and art as well as philosophy. Its function here is to organize the various and diverse activities of life and plural modes of judgment into a social and syndetic order. Religion establishes order within plurality—but it does so in part by fiat rather than query. Religion establishes general, comprehensive, and pervasive orders in human experience, but by generating permanent domains of mystery. To query, there is mystery everywhere, but nothing is impenetrable to further judgment with any modality. Philosophy is query predominantly in the mode of syndetic judgment. Religion is syndetic judgment in the service of another mode—usually active judgment. Religion provides comprehensiveness for life: but it is not a mode of query. Theology is syndetic discursive judgment, but it is limited in its range of interrogation. Theology and religion take certain mysteries for granted whose intransigence and impenetrability are definitive. There is no impenetrable mystery for query— though there are always unpenetrated mysteries which remain for further judgment.

IV.

ORDINAL PLURALISM

W̶e come, finally, to the theory of mystery, having considered some of the ways in which mystery pervades philosophy. Mystery, I have argued, is relevant throughout all philosophical undertakings, at their periphery if not their center, and has been recognized in some of its particular manifestations by a great many philosophers. What is required now is a theory of mystery that explains its sources and its properties, and which locates it in relation to other forms of understanding as well as philosophy. The only theory that adequately explains the qualities of mystery, I claim, is an ordinal metaphysics with its related theory of rationality and intelligibility. In such a theory, the origins and nature of philosophical mystery are a consequence of both the nature of things and the nature of philosophy. Mystery is the offspring of ordinal plurality, and the most successful approaches to mystery are those which welcome plurality, affirming its openness to rationality.

The mysteries I have considered are all mysteries in which indeterminateness plays a central role, particularly the multiplicity of determinations relevant to philosophic considerations. The history of philosophy may well be thought of as the recurrent attempt to ascertain some domain of reality which is entirely determinate. It may also be thought of as a continual unfolding of the indeterminateness in every determination. Mystery is clearly the outcome of indeterminateness, in knowledge and in being. But it is equally a function of determinateness, since complete indeterminateness is unintelligible, not mysterious at all. As a

66

consequence, an understanding of mystery depends on an understanding of the complementary interrelationship of determinateness and indeterminateness.

I will briefly sketch the categories and principles of an ordinal theory as a preface to the theory of mystery. A more detailed account can be found in my *Transition to an Ordinal Metaphysics* and, with some important differences, in Justus Buchler's *Metaphysics of Natural Complexes*. I will argue that such a theory makes mystery intelligible and rational, and shows how reason is interrelated with mystery as determinateness and indeterminateness are complementarily related. In this sense, mystery is one facet of the theory of judgment that is coordinate with an ordinal metaphysics.

The categories of an ordinal theory may seem somewhat arcane, yet they express certain fundamental features of the theory of mystery, which cannot be understood without them. Mystery is a function of indeterminateness — but an indeterminateness which is complementary with and inseparable from determinateness. Mystery is also a function of plurality — but a plurality of identities and relations in which determinateness is fundamental. Each of the pairs of categories of an ordinal theory expresses a complementary relationship of determinateness and indeterminateness, limitation and inexhaustibility. Each of the categories also expresses not a *kind* or *type* of being, distinct from all others, but a *function:* a way in which one order is relevant to another. Mystery can be understood in no other way. It is rooted in the ordinal character of our surroundings and our understanding of the plurality, functionality, and inexhaustibility of every ordinal relation.

Ordinality

Whatever is in any way is an order of constituents; every order is a constituent of other orders. The order-constituent relation is central to the ordinal theory: every constituent is related to its superaltern order; every order is related to its subaltern constituents. Here relatedness means relevance: whatever is relevant

67

to an order is one of its constituents. Reciprocally, however, if an order is relevant to another, one of its constituents, the second is relevant to the first. Nevertheless, though relevance and relatedness are complementary and mutual, there are two modes of relevance, and each of a pair of related orders may be relevant to the other in quite different ways. Every order functions both unitarily and plurally in every location, as a single order or constituent and throughout a range of relevant ramifications and influences. Some of its constituents are relevant specifically to its unitariness and singularity, others to its pervasiveness and ramifications. These comprise two different modes of relevance. However — this is a fundamental principle of the ordinal theory — not every order is relevant to, a constituent of, any given order. An order is a sphere of relatedness comprised of its constituents and their multiple relations, and has definite limits and boundaries.

Some examples may be helpful, though the generality of the categories must be maintained: whatever is is an order but also a constituent of other orders; whatever is relevant to an order is one of its constituents. Here, then, every physical object — rocks and stars, but also tables and hammers, works of sculpture and musical compositions — are all orders, along with numbers, theories, fictions, social institutions, processes, and hallucinations. Whether or not we want to say that any of these *exist,* they are relevant to other orders and are constituted by other orders: they inhabit spheres of relevance. Not only the atoms and molecules comprising a rock are its constituents, but the wind and rain that formed its shape, the natural events that caused its extrusion, the various properties it possesses, all are relevant to it and are included among its constituents. So are the animals and processes to which it contributes: the bear who sleeps on it in the sun, the family whose view is dominated by it, the hiker who takes shelter under it. Nevertheless, not every order is relevant to every other: every order has limits and boundaries. Elephants in Africa, seals in Antarctica, very large numbers, all would be irrelevant to a rock in New Hampshire unless it had had an extraordinary and varied history. Likewise, small events in remote

68

galaxies are irrelevant to events on our planet even if the galaxies themselves are related by gravitational and other influences. Relevance is not in general a transitive relation.

Influence and relevance are always mutual since they include whatever contributes to an order's sphere of relatedness, its relationship with other orders. Nevertheless, a house built on a rock, given shape by the rock, is related to it differently from the bear who could bask on another rock instead. Some constituents comprise what an order is, unitarily and characteristically, in a given location; others comprise its wider sphere of relevance and pervasiveness. There are two different modes of relevance involved, which I call respectively *integral* and *scopic relevance*. All of the categories of an ordinal theory define particular and complementary ways in which orders are related to each other as constituents.

The principle that there are only orders and their constituents in manifold and complex interrelations is a principle of *ontological parity:* no reality is more fundamental or more real. Every order is simply an order—not more or less so than any other. Constituents are orders themselves. Every order is a constituent of other orders. It follows that all claims to ontological priority— that any mode of being is more basic, fundamental, or primary— are arbitrary and untenable. There are no perfect simples, since such a simple would stand in no relations. There can only be simplicity of a particular kind, in a particular respect. There is nothing which is completely determinate; it is indeterminate relative to orders which intersect with it and engender possibilities for it. There is nothing which is wholly indeterminate, since it is what it is. Finally, there is nothing which is all-encompassing, for there is no order which includes all other orders.

If an order is said to have a specific and definite nature for all of its relations, we assign it a character for the world as a totality. To say that a being has an unqualified essence is to assign it a location in the world relative to all other beings. Ordinal pluralism entails that no being has *an* essence but many—characters expressing that being's relations to other orders of which it is a constituent. An unqualified essence commits us to a world order in

69

which all beings have one role. If every order is a constituent of many other orders—the fundamental principle of ordinal pluralism—it plays different roles relative to these different orders. Being here, along with identity and reality, is always qualified, relative to ordinal location.

Ordinality is a functional notion: *what* an order is is a function of the particular orders in which it is located. This functionality is manifested clearly in the different characteristics that an object possesses in and out of human life: a rock in the forest, taken home and used as a centerpiece of the garden, moved indoors as a doorstop, made a part of a found work of sculpture and exhibited in a museum. Not only does the rock possess new properties in every case in virtue of its new relations: its constituents are different and are related to it differently in these different orders. The bear who lived near it in the forest is no longer relevant to it in the museum; particular spatial configurations and patterns become relevant instead, as do monetary and critical considerations.

Among the notions which are opposed by ordinality are unqualified simplicity, indivisibility, and self-subsistence; but the fundamental antagonism is directed against all forms of ontological priority—that there is a fundamental reality. Such a reality must be a permanent and intransigent mystery, pervaded by arbitrariness. No being is more of an order than another nor more of a constituent. I will argue that ontological priority is essentially equivalent to the principle that the world is in some sense one defined in terms of what is ontologically prior. It is a central feature of ordinality that the world is not one, that there are plural and diverse orders of differing comprehensiveness and pervasiveness. A corollary is that every order is inexhaustible in fundamental ways, plural and indeterminate. This is a profound source of mystery.

The inexhaustibility of every order is manifested most transparently in the functional plurality of ordinal locations. Not only are the constituents relevant to a given order varied and diverse— all the different characteristics and influences relevant to our rock in the forest—and variable as well with new relationships in

70

a changing ecological network, but entirely new constituents become relevant to the rock in different ordinal locations. Since the rock "is" a sphere of relevance comprised of its constituents in a given location, but also inhabits many different locations and may inhabit many more, depending on circumstances, there is no set of constituents that exhausts what it is. Human contexts and norms manifest this inexhaustibility strikingly: any order may be given wholly new properties by human contrivance. But man is not required for such inexhaustibility: natural processes manifest very different properties at different levels of organization and when located in different systems. The properties of the moon in the solar system and for a particular night plant in the jungle or beach dweller are very different and in many ways discoordinate.

One of the fundamental tenets of the theory of orders—the basis of its pluralism—is the principle that not all orders are related to each other. Indeed, a constituent of a given order may be unrelated to some of its other constituents. It follows that in general, relatedness is intransitive, and that transitivity is the special case. Consider the constituents of order B which is a constituent of order A. While *some* constituents of B are also constituents of A, and while A itself is a constituent of B, there will be constituents of B which are not related to A. A bear and a hiker may never enter each other's sphere of relevance. though they both take shelter under the same rock. Certain molecules, essential to the rock's composition, are irrelevant to any particular uses made of it by organic life. Intransitive relatedness is essential if pluralism is to be maintained: otherwise the world would comprise a single system of relations. On the other hand, interrelations in the theory of orders are of indefinite ramifications. It is essential to the theory that there is indefinite relatedness without total relatedness. This inexhaustibility is a fundamental source of mystery.

To say that whatever is is an order of many constituents and a constituent of many orders is to emphasize relatedness and plurality: to be is to be an order of constituents and the constituents comprise the order. Every order is at least doubly

71

relational: in its constituents and relative to the constituents of a superaltern order in which it is located. These two conditions are inseparable, for the constituents of an order are whatever is relevant to it in a particular location. Therefore, the superaltern order in which a subaltern order is located is also a constituent of the subaltern order. The hand is a constituent of the body, but the body is a constituent of the hand in being *its* body. We may represent the relevant distinction among kinds of constitution in terms of the concepts of *integrity* and *scope*: a constituent of an order is part of its integrity within a superaltern order if the unitary function of the subaltern order within the superaltern order depends on that constituent. All other constituents of the superaltern order to which the subaltern order is relevant comprise its scope. The shape of a stone is essential to its utility as a platform, but may not be relevant to its use as a weight. The shape is an integral constituent of the stone in one location but not in the other, where it is simply part of the scope. (In some locations, it may be no constituent at all, irrelevant—for example, where the elements comprising the stone are of sole relevance, as in certain mining operations.) The integrity of a constituent defines its unitary function; its scope expresses its ramifications. A modification in scope is not necessarily a modification in integrity; a modification in integrity always involves a modification in scope.

Integrity and Scope

The integrity of an order is what is indicated in saying that we have *an* order, *a* being. An order is many in possessing many constituents and in belonging to many orders. But insofar as it is one in any sense, any location, it possesses an integrity. Individuality is a function of integrity; identity is also—representing a gross or comprehensive integrity. But there is no all-encompassing, total integrity or identity for any order—for there is no all-encompassing order inclusive of all other orders.

Because every order is located in many other orders, some of which are closely related to each other and similar in many respects, it is often very difficult in practice to determine the integrity of an order in a given location, though in principle an order possesses an integrity for each of its locations. It is frequently difficult in practice to distinguish the integrity of an order from its scope—for example, distinguishing which of a rock's folds and crevices are essential to its use by animals in the forest and which are merely ancillary. It is also frequently difficult in practice to distinguish one integrity of an order in a given location from other integrities where there is a close functional relationship—for example, determining the range of vowel variations within a given dialect as contrasted with variations that belong to other dialects of the same general language. Moreover, the range of possible functions of a rock—ranging from ecological roles to found sculptures and chemical materials—affords no common identity over all its integrities; the potential for phonological and grammatical variation over time gives us no comprehensive integrity defining the characteristics of a given language over all regional variations and linguistic developments.

All ordinal modes of relevance are minimally ternary, including integrity and scope. What this means is that the ways in which constituents belong to an order are functions of the location of this order in other orders. Even so-called universals vary in their essential properties depending on ordinal location: most painters know very clearly how the properties of perceived colors vary remarkably depending on their proximity to other colors, vary in subtle, complex, but often fundamental ways. This ternary complexity is the basis for the interconnectedness essential to both rationality and individuality. The integrity of an order B is comprised of those constituents C_i which are relevant to or define the function of B within some order A. Since B is always plurally located, it possesses many integrities; every order possesses many integrities.

An order is not its integrity and should not be confused with it. Every order possesses a scope corresponding to each of its integrities. A rock in the forest serves many organisms, leaves an indentation in the moist earth, shades certain plants—all effects of the rock but not essential to its function, not part of its integrity, in its role in the forest. To be a rock is to have many effects, to possess a comprehensiveness and pervasiveness, a scope, expressing the ramifications of that integrity in the relevant superaltern order. A rich work of art, which possesses a very complex integrity, nevertheless always produces a great number of effects, inhabits a wider sphere of relations, than can be included within that integrity. Integrity expresses what we mean in speaking of *an* order; but because integrity involves ternary relations, the scope is directly implicated. If B is located in A, then both A and some of its other constituents must be constituents of A. Those other constituents of A that are relevant to B insofar as it has an integrity in A comprise its scope. In other words, whatever else in the forest that is relevant to the rock, or to which it is relevant, that is not part of its integrity comprises its scope in the forest: the animals that use it but which do not affect its role, the shade it gives, and so forth.

The integrity and the scope of an order together define its function as a constituent in a superaltern order: the integrity its unitary function; the scope its plural relations to other constituents of the superaltern order—its pervasiveness or comprehensiveness in that order. What the rock is, in a given location, is comprised in the larger sense of all its constituents—integral and scopic. The integrity of an order represents that and how many constituents may function as one in a superaltern order. The scope of the order represents its plural ramifications in a particular location. A modification in integrity always involves a modification in scope, but not conversely. Integrity and scope *together* define the nature of a constituent within an order.

Relative to its integrity, an order's scope is partly indeterminate, for it is a function of the superaltern order's constituents in which it has that integrity. Relative to this integrity and the superaltern order, the scope is entirely determinate—a function of wider ordinal interrelations. The point is that indeterminateness and determinateness are doubly inseparable: they are both relevant in every ordinal location; moreover, their distinctiveness is only functional. What is determinate is indeterminate in certain respects. Conversely, whatever is indeterminate is determinate

74

in certain respects—that is, determinate in other ordinal locations, from another ordinal point of view. This complexity is the foundation of mystery, both its pervasiveness and its rationality.

Gross Integrity and Identity

An order has an integrity for each of its ordinal locations, and different integrities for different locations. Under certain conditions, in certain ordinal locations, many of these integrities functionally comprise a single gross integrity. This is the sense in which an order is "the same" over its many different locations. In all the examples given above, an order possesses a gross integrity over many different locations insofar as we can identify it at all: a rock is the same at different times, in different places, for different persons. The variation of integrity with different locations does not make a common identity obscure. So also. that a given tool—a hammer, for example— has many different kinds of uses, some of which are unexpected and atypical, is not incompatible with a single hammer being used and apprehended throughout these different employments.

Where there is a clustering of constituents $(C_i)_a$ of an order B_a, $(C_j)_b$ of order B_b, and so forth, where B_a, B_b, . . . are different integrities of B insofar as B is a constituent in different orders A_a, A_b, . . . , and where there is a superaltern order A comprising A_a, A_b, . . . such that the integrities of B are functionally related comprising one integrity in A, we have a gross integrity of B interrelating the integrities B_a, B_b, . . . This gross integrity is the basis for the identity of B within A among the constituent orders A_a, A_b, ... Integrity is a ternary relation; identity is a tetradic relation functionally unifying many integrities as constituents of a single integrity within a particular superaltern order. Every gross integrity is an integrity relative to some order; every integrity is a gross integrity relative to some order. There is no absolute identity of B, no intrinsic identity of B, for that would entail a world order. With no world order, there are only relative identities and no absolute or final identities. Identity and integrity are functional. They are the result of interrelations among

75

orders and natural interconnections.

The absence of a comprehensive, total identity for any order is a fundamental principle of the ordinal theory. It is difficult to exhibit by example, since the very consideration of a single order with different integrities manifests a common identity. The force of the example of the rock in the forest, placed within a museum, emphasizes how it can function in different locations with different integrities, but maintaining a functional relation among them. Similarly, Julius Caesar was not only a Roman general and ruler, writer and lover, but has been written about and utilized as example and subject of drama and stories, by name and indirectly. Nevertheless, given the wealth of roles he has been assigned throughout history, no integrity can encompass what Julius Caesar is, in all his different integrities. This is what inexhaustibility means. No comprehensive integrity can functionally relate all the roles Julius Caesar plays in all his different locations. Rather, there are many gross integrities of any order, comprising functional families of integrities with different degrees of overlapping.[1] No integrity, in no comprehensive order, can include all the diverse integrities of any order. No set of locations, however manifold, can exhaust the locations and traits of any order. There is a fundamental indeterminateness inherent in every order, its inexhaustibility over inexhaustibly many different locations.

Is it not then a fundamental mystery as to what any order is? There is no final account, no absolute identity. Identity is functional and relational. The identity of an order is qualified by its relations to other orders. This is the persistent and inescapable mystery of ordinal pluralism, and leads inevitably to mysteries of the world. The identity of an order is determinate only in a particular perspective, and there is no world-perspective.

Is it not also a mystery that there are orders — that is, that there is identity and integrity among orders? I think not. To be is to be an order — to have constituents and to be located in other orders, to possess integrities and scopes. What is mysterious is that orders possess the comprehensive identities we find them to have. The world might have been far more chaotic than it is, with narrower spheres of identity and relevance. In this sense, every

76

limit, every determination, has something mysterious within it — though it is a mystery that can be dissolved relative to some ordinal standpoint, which is then itself mysterious.

Prevalence and Deviance

We come now to ordinal categories which express stability and variation, typicality and atypicality. These are the categories of *prevalence* and *deviance*, and once again express a close complementary relationship of determinateness with indeterminateness, in certain respects and ordinal locations. A constituent is prevalent within an order to the extent that it is typical and restrictive, to the extent that subaltern orders in which it is located preserve its gross integrity in a superaltern ordinal location. It prevails in the sense of maintaining its identity through subaltern division.

In other words, an order prevails to the extent that it has a gross integrity in an ordinal location, and prevails throughout the orders whose integrities are comprised within that gross integrity. This is what "typicality" means: a rock prevails in its place throughout changing seasons and ecological transformations. A man, changeable in his emotions and personality, who plays different roles and adopts different personas to meet different circumstances, prevails throughout many different personalities and roles to the extent that a stable integrity comprises them all. Even change and transformation can prevail — as do the seasons and the tides, waves in the ocean, the expansion of the universe. Orders prevail when an integrity is pervasive throughout a range of subaltern ordinal locations.

Prevalences are stable and typical relative to their subaltern and superaltern orders. Deviances are also defined relative to subaltern and superaltern orders, but in terms of variations and departures. The number -1 is deviant relative to the orders of negative and positive integers: it prevails in the negative integers, but is deviant relative to the positive integers. Its integrity relative to the positive integers differs markedly from its integrity relative to the negative integers, yet the two systems of integers comprise a single order in which the number -1 prevails. What is deviant in one order is always prevalent in another order. The converse—that what is prevalent in one order is always deviant in another—may seem more difficult to establish.[2] Yet it is a straightforward consequence of the principle that there is no total identity for any order, no unqualified sense in which it is identical over all its different locations and integrities. A rock, prevalent in a location over many seasons and throughout changing conditions, has a different integrity for organisms that merely pass it by, for those that live within it, and for men who may use it as the foundation of a house or worship it as holy. Use, worship, and experimentation typically involve novel integrities and deviances. So does the plurality of ordinal locations relative to every order, which is the foundation of all prevalences and deviances.

What is prevalent in an order may not in the same respect be deviant in that order, and what is deviant is not in that respect prevalent—though what is deviant within an order may thereafter prevail there. A prevalent constituent of an order is typical relative to the order and some of its subaltern orders. In this respect, prevalence is also a ternary relation involving an order, a superaltern order, and certain subaltern orders functionally interrelated. A deviant constituent admits of divergent integrities within one superaltern order, relative to certain subaltern orders located within it. In this respect, prevalence and deviance are exclusive and complementary categories expressive of one of the fundamental forms of determinateness conjoined with indeterminateness. What is prevalent is typical and stable, determinate in that sense in a particular location. What is deviant is atypical, indeterminate in that location. Yet what is prevalent in one location is deviant in another and conversely.

Whatever exists or is in any way prevails in some order and is deviant relative to another. Even processes and beginnings prevail—in nature, for example. Nevertheless, whatever becomes or enters the world is deviant relative to some order. And there are deviances that are in no sense becomings. I have mentioned the number -1. Also, the Rocky Mountains are deviant relative to the Colorado plains. The mountains begin at the edge of the plains while they prevail in Colorado. Both prevalence and deviance are fundamental ways of belonging to orders: prevalence restrictive within an order relative to certain subaltern orders, deviance expressing the diversity of subaltern orders relative to each other.

Is prevalence another name for being? In one respect the answer is affirmative: whatever is in any respect prevails in some order. But since prevalence is ordinal and relational, not every important relation among constituents and orders is expressed by prevalence. Moreover, deviance is also a mode of being. Whatever is in any respect is deviant in some order. Being is not to be associated with prevalence alone. Rather, prevalence and deviance are two complementary, fundamental, and functional modes of being. Their complementary interrelationship is one of the fundamental sources of mystery: deviances amidst every prevalence.

Ordinality and Non-Being

Can an order fail to be? The question quickly becomes, can an order fail to be an order?—which is absurd. There are other interpretations: a prevalence can cease to be a prevalence in certain orders—though it cannot *altogether* cease to prevail. A deviance can cease to be deviant in an order by becoming prevalent there or by ceasing to be a constituent of that order—though it must be located in some order. An order cannot altogether cease to be an order. If there is no unqualified being in the theory of orders, there is certainly no unqualified non-being.

Not to be is elliptical—but no more so than, and quite like, the ellipsis of *to be*. In the sense in which to be is to prevail, not to be is not to prevail in a particular order. Can we speak of failing to prevail in any or all orders? There are several reasons why this is not intelligible, but the most obvious is that there is no all-encompassing order, therefore, no sum of orders relative to which there may or may not be a total prevalence. God, Zeus, the Furies, all prevail in some orders—if only myths and dreams.

79

There may be orders which prevail only in one man's imagination; there are orders which prevail only in discourse. But there is no total non-prevalence, unqualified non-prevalence. There is only relative non-prevalence: failing to be located in a particular order. Not to be is never *nothingness*: even a void prevails relative to its character and its surroundings. *Total non-being* is a mere juxtaposition of words.

It is therefore not possible for there to be no orders at all—especially if this means that an order is not an order. An order cannot fail to be an order. As for whether there might have been nothing at all—the mystery of existence has no meaning relative to ordinality. In order for there not to have been orders, there would have been other orders. There might, of course, have been orders with very different constituents than the ones there are. Even so, this relative non-being too is qualified, from some ordinal standpoint. The mysteries that owe their significance to absolutes and lack of qualification are dissipated from an ordinal point of view.

In modern times it has been fashionable to speak of appearances independent of any reality, as if only appearances might be real. This may be contrasted with more traditional conceptions where appearances are distinguished sharply from the reality for which they are surrogate. An appearance is real, but it passes for another reality. Such a complex mode of relevance is typical within the theory of orders. An appearance is an order which is similar enough to another order to be taken for it or pass for it. The epistemic function of appearance is to be one order and to pass for another. The ontological condition upon which this function is based is that of gross integrity. One order is not another order, yet the two may have the same integrity in one order and different integrities in other orders. Mislocation is likely where there is such an interplay of common and divergent integrities, and any order may be mislocated. Non-being is therefore the functional equivalent of appearance. Not to be is not to be located here but there. To appear is not to be one kind of order but to be another kind. There is no ontological distinction between appearance and reality, nor being and non-being.

Ontological Parity

From the standpoint of ordinality, there are only orders and constituents. Constituents are orders; orders are constituents of other orders. It follows that there is no ontological category of the "more real," the "fundamental," or the "ultimate." All modes of relation among orders and constituents are functional. Though there are indefinite numbers and kinds of orders, all are equally real—for all prevail somewhere and somehow. The traditional ways in which ontological priority is described—the ontologically fundamental, the really real—are acceptable distinctions within and relative to some superaltern orders. But they cannot be unqualified distinctions relative to a world order, for there is none.

Another way of putting this is that there is no generic, unqualified mode of priority. All attempts to define ontological primacy fail in not being general enough, in masking qualifications, in arbitrariness. All forms of alleged primacy can be shown to be arbitrary and limited in their range of adequacy. What is simple has been thought primary in that it is constitutive of aggregates while they are not constitutive in return. The principle of priority here seems to be one of dependency: what is more real is independent; what is less real is dependent. Nevertheless, there can be no total simplicity, for that would be total unrelatedness. There can be nothing simple in all respects; there is always multiplicity in unity. Sense-data, monads, indivisible forms, and substances may all be simple in some respect, but all are complex in having manifold relations. Forms have many instances. Simple impressions enter into many aggregates. What is most simple in one respect is usually most complex in its potentiality for aggregation.

The notion that what is independent is more real than what is dependent has its own difficulties. If we are speaking of causal dependency, then causes are more real and first causes are made intransigent mysteries. Far worse, dependency is a relative notion. If a particular instance is dependent on the form of which it is an instance, the form is dependent upon instances for its activity and manifestations. Where one being is dependent upon another for its essence, the second is dependent upon the first for its accidents. The integrity of an order is dependent both on a specified set of constituents and also on an ordinal location in a superaltern order. The superaltern order is dependent upon the subaltern order as well—there is mutual dependency. The subaltern orders or constituents of the integrity of an order are part of and dependent upon it for their scope. Finally, it may be argued that the character of any individual depends on other beings up to and including the entire universe. Only the entire totality of things is fully real. Now ordinality entails that there is no order of nature, no total order of the world, It is immediately apparent that dependency will not serve as an ontological criterion.

Other general criteria have been made the basis for ontological primacy: determinateness, range, breadth, and so forth. What is more determinate is said to be more real than what is less determinate. Nevertheless, many philosophers have claimed the opposite: that the ambiguous, global, and indeterminate is more real, perhaps because it is wider in scope. Ordinality entails that the scope of an order is always relative to a superaltern order, never relative to the entire universe, never unqualified and unconditioned. Nothing can be entirely or wholly determinate in all respects. Something entirely indeterminate could not be said to be at all—it would be no order. Complete indeterminateness is either impossible and unintelligible or a form of determinateness in being *wholly* indeterminate. Complete determinateness is likewise impossible since it entails total unrelatedness. Determinateness is an ordinal concept and cannot serve as the basis of ontological priority.

There are two fundamental deficiencies relative to doctrines of ontological priority. Both are forms of arbitrariness. First, there is the proposed criterion. I have discussed several, and could consider many more. Why is the simple more real than the complex? The latter is of greater richness and power. Why is the determinate more real than the indeterminate? The latter is a rich lode from which other modes of being can be mined.

Whitehead claims that only actualities are self-significant, as if self-significance were an obvious form of ontological primacy. But if everything is significant — either for itself or for another — why is *self*-significance more fundamental? Why are not pure possibilities more real in being significant *only* for others? Schematized in this way, there is an arbitrary preference that seems to ground most notions of ontological priority. Whatever one man selects as primary, another may treat as secondary.

Second, the notions which are the basis of ontological priority are arbitrary in their analysis and application. There is no unqualified simplicity, no unqualified determinateness, not even mere or unqualified self-significance. There is simplicity — but only in one or another respect, and accompanied by complexity in other respects. There is determinateness, but always accompanied by indeterminateness in certain respects. There is individuality, but only in the context of relatedness and multiplicity. From a general — that is, ontological — perspective, all these concepts represent functional relations among and within orders.

The theory of orders is committed to a principle of ontological parity: all orders are real; all orders are equally real. More important, reality — like all general concepts — is ordinal and relational. An order is real relative to certain orders and an appearance relative to others. Insofar as an order prevails, it is real; insofar as an order fails to prevail, it is not real — in a given location, in that particular respect. There is also the reality of deviance. The pluralism of ordinality makes ontological primacy unintelligible and indefensible.

The Inexhaustibility of Orders

The principle of ontological parity and the principle of inexhaustibility — that there is no world order — are in appropriate contexts equivalent. It is easy enough to show that a principle of ontological priority entails that there is a world order, for a given order can be held unqualifiedly more real or fundamental only relative to the world taken as a whole. To say that something is unqualified in any respect whatsoever is to assume a world

83

relative to which it bears this unqualified character.

The converse is that ontological parity entails the absence of a world order. Here I must add a qualifying premise: that there is a rich and complex world. Were there but one being in the universe, or even only a few, each might be as real as the others, yet there might be the world order of their aggregation. Now the notion that there might be but one being or order is incoherent. Were it a physical being, in what would it be located? Space and time would be other beings (or orders). There is also the number one (with the other numbers, perhaps all the orders of mathematics). Can there be one being without the entire system of integers? Without the real and complex numbers? The premises which permit us to imagine the prevalence of but one being turn out to contradict the hypothesis. Ontological parity entails that all orders have equal ontological status including physical objects, numbers, spaces, and so forth. Given many disparate kinds of orders, how could they be coordinated in a total order without a principle of ontological priority which designates many modes of prevalence unreal, "non-existent"—at least "less real," "derivative"?

The principle of inexhaustibility is therefore effectively equivalent to the principle of ontological parity. The two principles define the basis of ordinal pluralism—which may then be represented in terms of either the absence of a world order or the equal ontological status of all orders. Ordinal pluralism is faced with constant challenges to organization and comprehension, achieved in part but never completely. This is the basis of all mysteries in judgment. The project of eliminating indeterminateness and doubt, of dispelling mystery, is permanent and ongoing, not merely because we are finite creatures in an infinite universe, but because orders are indeterminate in many respects, and we are continually engaged in determining them in certain ways. Every such determination has a price in indeterminateness. Human experience testifies recurrently to increasing problems as an outcome of implemented solutions. Nothing in our ordinal surroundings is entirely determinate. This is the foundation of mystery.

84

To emphasize the principle of the inexhaustibility of orders, we may consider the question of the nature of the physical world. The inexhaustibility of nature is due in part to the inexhaustible plurality of modes of being: everyday objects, atoms, and galaxies, but also numbers, algebras, historical beings, fictional histories, times, places, constructed spaces and times in works of art, and so forth. These diverse modes of being cannot all be conjoined under one all-encompassing system. They cannot all be related to one inclusive order. Each is interrelated with others, but not all are related to each other or to any other single order.

But is there a physical world, a world of space and time? Can we at least identify a total order of material events and beings? Or does the inexhaustibility of orders pervade every order, so that there is no material world (nor a mental world)? *The physical world* is as mistaken a notion as *the universe altogether.* The difficulty in both cases is the same: of determining the boundaries of the relevant superaltern order. The universe as a whole cannot be given all orders as constituents. They do not comprise a collectivity. Analogously, what belongs in the physical world? Tables and chairs, hammers and machines created by men? In addition to atoms and molecules, do we include waves and energy? Energy and radiation are not material themselves, but they have important causal and explanatory functions relative to events. Atoms are not solid matter, but they are basic to physical explanation. What of space and time or space-time? What of the curvature of the earth? Is it physical? Not in a narrowly literal sense. Yet it is certainly a constituent of the physical world. Now, is there any kind of order which does not exert an influence on physical events through the mediation of men? Numbers and mathematical relations influence mathematicians and physicists. Musical works inspire men to music and to important activities with physical consequences. Works of literature have a moral and behavioral influence. And so forth. "The physical world" cannot be restricted to solid, substantial beings and still play its explanatory role in the physical sciences. Once the door is opened to wider constitutive relations, everything breaks in.

Either the physical world is too narrow for science and utility, therefore arbitrarily defined; or else it is everything—which is effectively nothing, since all things cannot be taken together. Here is another important principle of mystery: that all orders are related to other orders, but not all orders are related to every other. There are the mysteries of openendedness, interrelations without end. There are also the other mysteries of unrelatedness, limitations, of gaps and the absence of mediation.

Possibilities and Actualities

Given an order, some of its constituents are actualities and some are possibilities. In this respect, actuality and possibility represent modes of ordinal location. We may say further that the possibilities *belong* to the actualities. Possibility is another ternary relation among orders and constituents—though quite different from others discussed above. The actualities of an order possess possibilities by virtue of the order's extensions or interrelations with other orders. For example, rain is a possibility given a low barometric pressure system and certain climatic conditions. It is a possibility *of* or *for* these actual conditions as relevant within a future order. Temporal possibilities reflect the extension of an order with a temporal location into similar orders at other times. Nevertheless, not all possibilities are temporal or involve time even indirectly. Given the actualities of the continuum of real numbers, it is a possibility: (a) that there are eleven coins in a drawer—here a possibility belonging to the actual numbers and the actual drawer; (b) that numbers may be located as points on a line; and (c) that two triangles containing sides equal to ten and three and an angle of thirty degrees are congruent. Non-temporal possibilities reside in all works of art, all human judgments. In every case, possibilities in an order belong to the actualities of that order relative to the interplay between that order and other orders.

The four defining conditions distinguishing actualities from possibilities may now be mentioned:

(a) *Possibilities belong to actualities*. The sense involved is what Aristotle has in mind when he claims that activities and potentialities belong to primary substances or individuals. The difference is that there is no ontological priority involved, for possibilities are as "real" as actualities— indeed, what is possible in one order is actual within another; and what is actual within one order is a possibility in another. Natural laws are both actualities and possibilities: actual regulative conditions of instances of a common kind; possibilities for events with recurrent actualizations. When we say that actualities belong to possibilities—as we might claim that possible rain is actually wet or the law of gravitation is actually an inverse square law—we transform the orders involved and regard the possibility as an actuality: actual rain is actually wet; the actual law has an actual structure. Technically speaking, possibilities belong to the scope of their actualities but do not belong to their integrity, while the actualities to which a possibility belongs belong to its integrity. The possibility of rain tomorrow is part of the scope of conditions today, but the conditions today belong to the integrity of rain tomorrow insofar as it is a possibility for today. That is, the rain is a possibility only in terms of today's conditions. Both today's conditions and the rain tomorrow are actualities in other orders.

(b) *Possibilities are always plural relative to any actual conditions.* It is important to distinguish this principle from the indefinite plurality of orders relative to their constituents and their ordinal locations in superaltern orders. Possibilities are not only many, but are plural *alternatives* within an order. There are two different kinds of relations among the constituents of an order: given a set of (actual) constituents, other constituents of the order may be strictly determined without prevailing alternatives. Given litmus paper in acid, its color is settled. But given the actual conditions of an order, alternative possibilities always prevail. If it is possible that it will rain tomorrow, it is also possible that it will not rain. If it is a possibility within a novel that the hero will be killed, it is also a possibility that he will not. Possibilities carry the weight of alternatives relative to established actual conditions. Determinism is equivalent to the thesis that there are only actualities, that there are no possibilities. The prevalence of possibilities

87

is sufficient to provide a ground for mystery, indeterminism, novelty, and freedom.

The condition of plural possibilities lends itself to a more specific formulation:

(c) *In any given location, possibilities prevail as logically incompatible alternatives while actualities must be logically compatible.* Logically diverse actualities may prevail in a given order — for example, circles and squares both prevail in the order of geometrical objects, while no being can be both a circle and a square. Nevertheless, circles and squares either do not represent alternatives which prevail together for some actuality, or they are possibilities rather than actualities. Where prevalences represent diverse alternatives, they are possibilities.

This condition taken by itself is the foundation of logical possibilities: whatever is logically compatible with defining conditions is regarded as possible. The trouble with logical possibilities is that they are relative only to orders in discourse radically simplified relative to prevailing conditions. For example, it is a logical possibility that a pumpkin might turn into a coach — but not a possibility in the order of pumpkin farming. Logical possibilities are only vaguely located in orders, and their lack of precise location leads to two errors: (1) What is possible is detached from the prevailing conditions of prevailing orders. Logical possibilities do not reflect the specific integrities of specific orders in specific locations, but hover unattached to their actualities. In addition, (2) logical possibilities are generated in discourse and belong to discourse, not to actualities resident in other ordinal locations. It is a logical possibility that flowers might speak and think when planted in sufficiently hard ground — but not a possibility for flowers grown in ordinary gardens. Fanciful possibilities belong to actualities in artistic orders; other possibilities prevail in very different orders. Condition (a), interpreted ordinally, avoids the emptiness attaching to logical possibilities.

Conditions (a), (b), and (c) define the distinctions and relations among actualities and possibilities. The remaining condition is not a distinguishing condition, but a principle relating possibilities to ordinal pluralism. It is a central principle at the heart of mystery.

(d) *In every order possibilities prevail as well as actualities.*
Were everything actual, there would be a single, all-encompassing, actual order. This is quite independent of temporality.
Nevertheless, if there were no alternatives for the future, the
world would comprise a total, actual order. The sense in which
the future would be indeterminate would not include future alternatives or possibilities, only the limited, temporal location
of our consciousness. There would be a four-dimensional, actual
continuum. The central meaning of the indeterminateness of the
future refers to the prevalence of genuine possibilities.

Possibilities prevail in every order by virtue of the ramified
interconnections among orders. There is a colloquial sense in
which we may say that an order and its actualities comprise its
self-sufficiency, what it actually is as an order. Nevertheless, the
actualities of an order are not equivalent with its integrity:
possibilities are often part of the integrity of an order, representing the powers of some of its constituents. Every order is
plurally located in many superaltern orders, and its plural locations, which define its plural integrities, provide it with plural
possibilities. For every order there are indeterminacies or alternatives represented by possibilities—though the possibilities
which prevail within an order are quite definite and determinate
as such. Even a self-sufficient, absolutely perfect God would
admit of the diverse possibilities which finite forms may take in
his universe.

Ordinality and Being

Four complementary pairs of functional categories are fundamental within the ordinal theory. These are order and constituent, integrity and scope, prevalence and deviance, possibility
and actuality. In every case, the two members of a pair express
closely related and complementary ways in which constituents
function in a particular ordinal location. In the most obvious case,
we have orders and constituents. Yet it is important to emphasize
that every order has constituents and is itself a constituent of
other orders. Moreover, these two conditions are closely related

89

since the constituents an order possesses are a function of its ordinal location, of its role as a constituent in a superaltern order. The relevant constituents of a rock vary depending on whether it is located in the forest, in a home, or in a museum as a found work. Likewise, a given order "is" an order relative to its constituents, but it "is" a constituent relative to its location and function within other orders. It is both order and constituent inextricably and functionally, but in each case, is what it is by virtue of the sphere of relevance in which it is located. This is the ordinality upon which the theory is based.

The functionality and complementarity of the theory entail that being, like non-being, is always plural and relational. There is no unqualified sense of being or non-being. All of the categories express particular modes of being—particular ways in which orders function, for that is the only sense of being in an ordinal theory. Therefore, every order *is* both an order and a constituent: many orders and many constituents. To be, here, is to function in an ordinal location: as an order or as a constituent. There is an ambiguity, indeterminateness, or plurality intrinsic to being-an-order (or constituent) that is fundamental within the theory and perhaps the ultimate source of mystery. Being is always plural and qualified, and there is no absolute, wholly determinate, or unqualified sense of being, no sense inclusive of all the other senses of being.

An order, then, functions *as* an order, *is* an order, but also functions *as* a constituent, *is* a constituent. It also, in some of its ordinal locations, is a constituent of the integrity of another order, and in other locations, is a constituent of scope. Integrity, then, is also a mode of being: a way of functioning within an order; so is scope. Being here is thoroughly qualified and relational—minimally ternary in relation, involving at least an order, its constituents, and a superaltern order in which it is located. Analogously, prevalence and deviance are modes of being, ways in which a constituent functions within an order relative to a range of subaltern orders. Similarly, possibility and actuality are modes of being. Each pair represents a complementary but pervasive sense of being: every order functions somewhere as an order, elsewhere as a constituent, somewhere as prevalent, elsewhere as deviant, as integral and as scopic, as possibility and as actuality.

By the principles of ontological parity and inexhaustibility, there is no all-encompassing, total sense of being under which all these different senses may be coordinated. Being as ordinality is complemented by constituency and qualified by ordinal location. There is no comprehensive gross integrity inclusive of all other integrities of an order, for that would be incompatible with the pervasiveness of deviance along with prevalence. There is then a profound and systematic indeterminateness inherent in ordinality: the indeterminateness of a plurality of modes of being, none of which takes unqualified precedence over the others. Analogously, however, there is a determinateness inherent in every form of indeterminateness, for each category expresses a determinate mode of being.

In each of the fundamental pairs of categories, one member may be regarded as expressive of determinateness: order, integrity, prevalence, actuality. The other member may be regarded as expressive of indeterminateness: constituent, scope, deviance, possibility. An order regarded as an order has a specific range of constituents: "is" its constituents. But it is also located in many orders and has many constituents itself. "Order" expresses unity and integrity; constituency expresses plurality of location along with the indeterminateness of scope. The ramifications of an order are always wider than any integrity can determine. Likewise, every order prevails somewhere—with a stable gross integrity—and is deviant elsewhere—with variable integrities. Similarly, possibilities are indeterminate relative to actual conditions.

The functionality of being entails that determinateness is always complemented by indeterminateness, but also that indeterminateness is always complemented by determinateness, in an indefinite variety of ways. An order may be a constituent of many orders, but it possesses a gross integrity and prevails in many locations. An order deviant in some locations prevails in other locations. A possibility in one location is actual in other locations. If determinateness is qualified by an indefinite range of indeterminatenesses, the converse is equally true: indeterminateness is replete with determinateness. This complementary and reciprocal relationship is both the source of mystery and the resolution of its intransigence. Mystery is unending, but it is profoundly cognizable and analyzable, through all the modes of determinateness which are relevant to it.

Judgment

The theory of mystery is based on a pluralistic and ordinal theory of judgment. There are many modes of judgment as there are many modes of being, types of orders. The defining conditions of judgment are *interrogation* and *validation*. Judgments are responses to demands resident in conditions and circumstances to which standards of validation are applicable. Assertions provide true or false claims in response to questions posed. Actions are evaluated in terms of the control they provide within conditions and circumstances. Works are constructed, formed and produced, evaluated in terms of their distinctiveness and importance. The diversity of orders in experience is constantly brought under unifying systems of remarkable comprehensiveness. Assertion, action, construction, and comprehension are modes of judgment to which validation is central.

An important distinction for mystery is that between judgment and query. All judgments are interrogative, concerned with validation. When such judgment opens up into ongoing, unrestricted interrogation with methods for establishing validation throughout comprehensive spheres of human activity, we have query. Science, ethics, art, and philosophy are all modes of query; and that is their rational character.

Every mode of judgment is all-pervasive—that is, applicable to whatever can be judged. Assertions may be regarded as acts, creations, or components of comprehensive judgments; acts may be regarded as assertions about circumstances and needs, the creation of a style of life, or as a comprehensive way of organizing oneself relative to complex surroundings; constructions may be regarded as comments on circumstances, as deeds in response to circumstances, or as components of unified experience; a system of metaphysical categories may be regarded as a set of assertions about the world and experience, as a component of a full and good life, or as a created work. No judgment belongs to but one mode. In this sense, every judgment is multimodal; and where interrelated by virtue of comprehensive subaltern orders, judgments are also intermodal.

Intermodality is a strong condition of interconnection in judgment. I have noted that science is not assertive judgment alone — though it emphasizes that mode of judgment — but appeals to pragmatic, aesthetic, and systematic criteria to ground the validation of scientific theories. Science is a mode of query for which the various modes of judgment are *coordinate*: not merely plurally located relative to any judgment, but jointly constitutive of scientific validation. We must distinguish merely plural judgments from plural judgments which define a coherent and novel order. The question is whether intermodality may establish novel modes of judgment beyond the four I have distinguished. Is science to be distinguished as a mode of judgment from other kinds of assertion? *Prima facie,* it is as plausible to argue that science fulfills the imperatives of assertive judgment in a pluralistic world as that science attains a novel union of all the modes of judgment with an emphasis upon assertive judgment. Courts of law blend assertive judgments far more intimately with moral and political concerns. Everyday experience, it may be noted, is a hodgepodge of judgmental modality. Science, courts of law, and everyday experience may be distinguished on the basis of the integrities of the different modes of judgment within them.

Analogously, ethics, morals, politics, and everyday practice may be distinguished: everyday action establishes itself as correct within modest limits; politics and ethics may be regarded as forms of query where assertions and systematic considerations, institutions and traditions, play a vital role. Morals is practice in the light of ideals and obligations — yet it need not be query.

In the same way, art and constructive judgment may be distinguished. Constructive judgments may reside in domains

93

unsuitable for art—for example, moral. philosophical, and every-day judgment. Nevertheless, there are didactic works of literature and works with a moral purpose. Applied arts such as architecture, pottery, and dress inevitably emphasize intermodal contrasts—but they are not obviously less or inferior art. Religious art is to a moral and religious purpose; yet it is indistinguishable from art in the sense of query.

Finally, syndetic or comprehensive judgment is implicit in all great enterprises. Science seeks theories applicable to all objects and events; ethics seeks ideals applicable to all actions and events; politics seeks accommodation among all human interests; art attains works of great range and comprehensiveness, bringing together the most disparate elements of life and feeling. Nevertheless, there can be science, ethics, and art with a restricted purview. Only metaphysics emphasizes syndetic judgment predominantly and unrestrictedly as its supreme aim, employing assertions and constructions as means to its ends.

An essential characteristic of a mode of judgment or query is the prevalence of a typical and unique mode of validation. Science has technical modes of validation distinct even from other assertive claims and justifications. Nevertheless, we must emphasize ordinality: a judgment valid in one mode may be invalid in another, and there is no validation that is not ordinal. A scientific theory may be true but morally destructive. A great work of art may be based on untruths. Neither is flawed in its typical mode of validation, but may be flawed in others. There is no unqualified mode of validation.

Based on the foundations of ordinality and query, we may develop a theory of cognitive mystery. Yet the theory of orders and of multimodal judgment is not the cause of mystery, but its explanation. There has never been a philosophical explanation which was not fundamentally mysterious. Yet many philosophic mysteries have been intransigent, opaque. This, I am suggesting, is due to inadequate metaphysical and epistemological assumptions. The ordinal theory accommodates a theory of mystery in which rationality is coordinate with mystery, and the latter ceases to be intransigent and opaque. With this reminder, we may turn directly to the sources and nature of philosophic and other cognitive mysteries, rooted in the nature of things and in the nature of rationality.

V.

MYSTERY AND PHILOSOPHY

We enter here upon the task of determining the nature of philosophical mysteries. While all mysteries depend upon the limits of knowledge, there are at least four distinct possibilities: (a) there are mysteries because of the nature of things: they are ineffable, unfathomable; (b) there are mysteries because of the limitations of knowledge: there are questions which have no answers; (c) there are secrets and mysteries, but there is nothing intrinsically unknowable about what is kept secret; (d) there are mysteries because of the nature of things and the nature of knowledge, but nothing is intrinsically unknowable. Of the four alternatives, only the last is appropriate to the sense of mystery which has evolved out of our earlier considerations.

We might expect a detailed theory of knowledge to provide a basis for mystery. Yet most such theories transform mystery into scepticism. Alternatives (a) and (b), for example, equate scepticism and mystery: what cannot be known is mysterious because of the nature of things and the limits of knowledge. Alternative (d) relates mystery and knowledge by affirming that what is mysterious can be known and that knowledge is mysterious. I have made a presumptive case that knowledge neither is incompatible with mystery nor does it dispel mystery. I will strengthen the claim: mystery is a part of knowledge. The task of query is not to eliminate but to transform mystery.

96

The Origins of Mystery

In one sense, plurality is the source of mystery: the plurality of orders and of modes of judgment. The principle of inexhaustibility is an expression of plurality, though it must be extended to include the inexhaustibility of query. The principle of ontological parity is another such expression, though it must be supplemented by the principle of epistemic parity: that there is no supreme form of knowledge, no supreme mode of judgment. In the end, we may say that the cause of mystery is simply ordinality, understood in its full sense relative to the categories and principles which express it.

Yet the full sense of ordinality is difficult to explicate, and the causes of mystery may as readily be viewed as many as we have viewed them as one. "Ordinality" designates the most pervasive feature of our pluralistic ontology—and of the orders it characterizes. But ordinality is plural in the categories which express its ramifications; and it is inexhaustible. It behooves us to consider the causes of mystery in a detail sufficient to their complexity.

It is worth repeating that the ordinal theory is not a sceptical theory of mystery, but quite the reverse. The ramified plurality of orders and modes of judgment is the source of mystery—but of knowledge also. After discussing the origins and nature of mystery, I will consider the remarkable truth that mystery is the positive and constructive foundation of knowledge. It does not inhibit, but enhances reason. No flavor of absolute limits of reason is involved nor a pessimistic scepticism toward human powers except as limits are intrinsic to all orders. Such matters will be my final concern. I will proceed now with the causes of mystery.

All mysteries may be regarded as consequences of ordinality. For convenience, I will consider ordinality from the standpoint of three central characteristics, none of which is a technical category within the ordinal theory. These are *inexhaustibility, functionality,* and *complementarity.* All are profound sources of mystery.

97

(a) *Inexhaustibility.* Every order is inexhaustible. This means that every order is indeterminate in many ways, as it is determinate in many ways, and that no complete, exhaustive determination can express the nature of an order. This inexhaustibility is expressed by the categories of an ordinal theory in a variety of ways. For every integrity, an order has a scope including constituents not part of its integrity. Every order has many integrities, a different integrity for every ordinal location. Every order is deviant in certain respects and prevalent in other respects, possesses possibilities as well as actualities, and so forth. In sum, every determination is qualified and relational, from a point of view, and no point of view exhausts the world nor any particular order.

A corollary is that there is no order which is the entire world. There is no order of nature, not even an order of the physical world closed under causal relations. There is no order which comprises as its constituents all other orders. This principle is the foundation of an ordinal theory. Every order has plural ramifications. In particular, every order has plural integrities: therefore, the integrity of an order relative to one superaltern order is indeterminate in some respects relative to its other integrities. This is a major source of mystery. It is also expressed in the principle that possibilities prevail in every order—alternatives within that order relative to its relations with other orders.

My immediate concern is with the trait of inexhaustibility: that there is no order relative to which any other order is entirely determinate. Such determinateness, I am arguing, is intelligible only in term of a world order. Consider, now, the mystery of the world. Ordinality entails that there is no world whose existence is an ultimate mystery. We cannot seek the reasons for the existence of the world altogether—for there is no such world.

We may formulate the source of mystery given by inexhaustibility negatively: If there were not a plurality of mysteries, if there were not mysteries everywhere, that would entail an all-encompassing world order. There would then be the absolute mystery of the existence of the world. Spinoza's cosmology is the supreme expression of a world order predicated on an ultimate mystery which seeks to abolish every finite mystery. Yet Spinoza does not succeed: for there are profound mysteries related to the infinite attributes of God and the individual essences of finite modes. Given the ramified plurality of orders entailed by inexhaustibility, there is mystery everywhere — in every order and in its plural locations, for there is no ultimate location relative to a world order. There can be knowledge without mystery only in a cosmic world order. (As I will show, there can be no knowledge in such a world order, for query would be impossible and unintelligible.) Inexhaustibility is the source of the indefinite openness belonging to every order in its plural locations and determinations, and this is the source of plural mysteries.

(b) *Functionality.* Inexhaustibility is closely related to the relationality and functionality of orders — and especially, the functionality of every ordinal constituent and category. *What* an order is, here, is a function of its relations and constituents. There is no unqualified identity, no unqualified property. Every determination is relational and qualified. Every determination expresses how an order (or constituent) functions in an ordinal location, within a sphere of relevance. Inexhaustibility expresses the infinite range of qualifications and ramifications relevant to every order. But the mystery of ordinality is expressed even more directly by the functionality of ordinal relevance. To be, here, is to function in an order in certain ways relative to other orders and constituents. Every ordinal category expresses such a functional determination: not *kinds* of beings, but *functions* of orders in different locations.

The mystery here is apparent. There is no unqualified determination, only functional, relational determinations. Every order functions in many different ways in different locations, expressed in part by the multiplicity of its integrities and the complementarity of the ordinal categories as they apply to it. An order is a possibility in one location, an actuality in another; prevalent in one location, deviant in another; and so forth. This multiplicity of roles and determinations is a profound source of mystery.

(c) *Complementarity.* Functionality has a direct and immediate consequence, expressed in the complementary relationship

99

of pairs of ordinal categories: order-constituent; integrity-scope; prevalence-deviance; possibility-actuality. Each category is complemented by another. The pair together defines a mode of functioning in an ordinal location; but each member of a pair is complementarily related to the other, and entails the other. There are no possibilities in an order without actualities, and each is a joint function of other possibilities and actualities. What is prevalent in one location is deviant in another, and prevalence and deviance together define the interrelationship of the integrities of the constituents in a given order.

This condition is far stronger than what can be expressed in terms of conceptual tensions and bipolar oppositions. All too often a determination that involves its opposite is regarded as incoherent. Determinateness that entails indeterminateness is thought unintelligible. The notion of conceptual tension tends to restrict the origin of mystery to the understanding. An ordinal theory defines the interrelationship of determinateness and indeterminateness as a property of every order, inherent in the nature of things.

Inexhaustibility, functionality, and complementarity are all closely related concepts expressing fundamental features of ordinality. Ordinality is the ultimate source of mystery, and we may explore it further by a reexamination of the ordinal categories in their relationship to mystery.

(d) *Integrity and Scope.* The integrity of an order comprises a ternary relationship among constituents and orders; so does the order's scope. The integrity of an order represents its unitary function in an ordinal location relative to a superaltern order. The scope of the order is comprised of the other constituents of the superaltern order which are also constituents of the given order. Now since every order has plural locations, it follows that to know a given integrity of an order is not to know all its integrities. Even a gross integrity of an order among diverse subaltern integrities reflects only their capacity to serve as one in a particular superaltern order, not in all orders, and not in their diverse ramifications within that superaltern order. One relevant mystery has been noted: no integrity exhausts the nature of a given order. There are its other integrities. There is an in-determinateness to ordinal being that is the source of profound mysteries, especially in the mode of assertive judgment.

A related source of mystery is based on the connection between integrity and scope. A traditional philosophic error has been to identify a being with its essence. An analogous error would be to identify an order with its integrity; for it can only be the order it is, located in a particular superaltern order, relative to its scope. The integrity of an order represents its unitary function in a given location. Its scope represents its plural functions in the same order—and every order has both unitary and plural functions in a given location.

The scope of an order is indeterminate in certain respects relative to its integrity. The scope represents the fullness and pervasiveness of the order in one of its locations, and is comprised of the constituents of the superaltern order to which it is relevant in its functions. Suppose we could delineate all the constituents of the integrity of an order and its location in a given superaltern order. The scope would not be determined entirely by this integrity. The scope of an order expresses its openness to a wider range of interconnections than its integrity, for it is an expression of the range of constituents of the superaltern order.

I have given several examples of the relevant mysteries. The integrity of the number two in the system of numbers and arithmetic relations is given by all other numbers and relations among them. But the scope of the number two in human experience includes at least all pairs—and these are not determinable from the integrity of numbers nor from other known integrities. A kindly and generous man (his integrity) may nevertheless make others hate him by his kindliness: the hatred and harm he produces is part of his scope in social life. We are commonly aware that the integrity of an order does not suffice to give us its ramifications in any of its ordinal locations.

The mystery here is related to the view that to know something is to know everything. There is no world order, and everything cannot be known. Nevertheless, being always transcends knowledge with respect to both scope and possibilities. Both are

101

sources of mysteries that represent the limits of human capacity due to ordinal locations.

(e) *Prevalence and Deviance.* A constituent of an order prevails in that order insofar as it is restrictive relative to certain subaltern orders. Its integrity within the superaltern order is functionally identical with its integrity in the subaltern orders relative to which it is prevalent. Prevalence is therefore a function of interrelations among superaltern and subaltern orders. A constituent of an order is deviant in that order relative to subaltern orders in which it possesses a divergent integrity. Prevalence characterizes an order dominant relative to specific subaltern orders. Deviance characterizes an order insofar as it possesses divergent integrities over a range of superaltern and subaltern orders. Prevalences defines an order typically; deviance defines an order atypically.

Deviance is a function of what is typical in contrast with what is not, relative to related superaltern and subaltern orders. It follows that whatever knowledge we can gain of the prevailing constituents of an order, deviances will remain: whatever is typical among certain subaltern orders, there will be deviations relative to others. We might explore the plains forever, quite missing the mountains. The Grand Canyon is a remarkable and overwhelming deviance relative to the surrounding desert. The irrational numbers are deviant relative to certain arithmetic functions though prevalent with respect to others. The brute impact of novel experiences is an expression of their deviance. The mystery here is that there may be deviances which prevailing conditions do not reveal, and that even where deviances are encountered and apprehended, they depart from what typically prevails. The differences which are deviant are always mysterious in that what is prevalent does not include them.

A deviance is always mysterious relative to the prevailing constituents of an order though they may be compatible from the standpoint of another order. We overcome mystery and incongruity by moving from the narrower to a more comprehensive order. But where a given order represents the widest relevant sphere of relations for us—though not perhaps the widest prevailing or possible—it is and remains a mystery. An emergent quality—life—is deviant relative to prevailing inorganic conditions. These are so typical and prevalent in human life that our knowledge cannot entirely bridge the gulf. Deviances relative to the major and characteristic traits of human experience are inevitably mysterious.

(f) *Actuality and Possibility.* Actualities and possibilities prevail in every order. The constituents which are actual afford no alternatives in that order. We may colloquially call them "settled" relative to the prevailing integrities of that order. These actualities "have" possibilities in the sense that the constituents which are possibilities are not part of the integrity of their actualities while the actualities are part of the integrity of their possibilities. And the possibilities represent alternatives for these actualities— alternatives which prevail by virtue of the interrelations of orders. The distinguishing conditions of actuality and possibility are that (1) both actualities and possibilities prevail in every order; (2) possibilities belong to actualities; (3) wherever a possibility for an actuality prevails, other related possibilities also prevail for that actuality; (4) actualities may possess possibilities contradictory in the same respects, but actualities which are contradictory in the same respects cannot prevail in the same order.

Possibilities represent the plurality of orders and their relations relative to any one order—its open and plural interrelations with other orders. Possibilities also express the inexhaustibility of every order. Inexhaustibility and relatedness are global traits. From the standpoint of any order the two conditions establish possibilities. Possibilities represent the extension of an order into other orders: its actualities possess possibilities by virtue of the complex and indeterminate boundaries among orders. Even the scope of an order may be actual in part—for example, the pairs of socks in a drawer are actualities included in the scope of the number two in a man's experience. But there are also possibilities for each pair of being worn on a given day or of matching the color of a person's eyes. Wherever there are interrelated but distinct orders, there are alternative possibilities.

I have equated determinism with the principle that there are only actualities. This principle entails the prevalence of a world order in which all beings are actual. These conditions may be interpreted as equivalent to the principle that actuality is transitive: from any set of actualities and the interrelations of orders, we may extend actuality by transitive relevance to a totality of actualities relative to the universe as a whole. Therefore, the condition that there are possibilities in every order is equivalent with the principle that actuality has limits and boundaries which are sufficiently pervasive to engender possibilities in every order. Inexhaustibility, relatedness, possibility, and the intransitivity of relevance are all closely related.

Insofar as possibilities represent alternatives within an order by virtue of its plural relations, mysteries are inevitable. Let us take assertive judgment as a beginning. In assertive query we seek to establish a correspondence between an order of discourse and another order. Such a correspondence can be established only relative to the actualities of that order. In predicting a future eclipse, we establish given actual observations and actual scientific laws as a basis of prediction. We do not predict by virtue of possibilities, but relevant actualities. Assertive judgment seeks to establish actualities for all possibilities: it seeks to overcome inexhaustibility and ordinality.

Active judgment is the achievement of control by extension from given actual conditions through what is possible to new actual conditions. Action is a major source of possibilities in human experience—and also a major source of the transformation of possibilities into actualities: but never all possibilities. Possibilities haunt active judgments—alternatives which are not within our control. Failure is always a possibility, no matter what precautions are taken. The openness of orders and their complex and plural interrelations entail that action is always perilous and establish a permanent but constantly shifting gulf between deliberation and successful action. We say that there is a component of luck or fortune in every successful action; this is another name for the mystery of successful active judgment.

Constructive judgment is the creation of a novel order taking possibilities into account, reveling in them. In a sense, art as constructive judgment escapes mystery by affirming it and by meeting the plurality of possibilities by a plurality of imaginative conceptions and works. Nevertheless, the result is the plural mysteries of art — the art object, artistic value, the artist's intentions, plural interpretations, and so forth. Art often seems paradoxical because of the importance of alternative possibilities in every work and interpretation.

Actualities are amenable to knowledge in all forms of judgment. Even in constructive and syndetic judgment, the aim is to produce an actual work or system. Nevertheless, there are always plural possibilities for that work, as well as plural possibilities in orders that are not included within it. We expand a given order of discourse to a more comprehensive order so as to gain greater control. But possibilities always prevail — especially due to the inexhaustibility and functionality of orders; therefore, there are always limitations to judgment and knowledge. These are sources of mystery. Such mysteries are indefinitely open to further judgment, for possibilities are also actualities. Possibilities are knowable — but through prevailing actualities. There are then other possibilities which generate further mysteries without end.

(g) *Plural Modes of Judgment.* Corresponding to the plurality and inexhaustibility of orders, there is a plurality of modes of judgment. There is no all-encompassing world order; there is no supreme mode of judgment or kind of knowledge. I have identified query with rationality, but query takes many forms and has no supreme form. The consequences of such an epistemic plurality must now be traced. It is inevitable that modal plurality of judgment should engender mystery. I have discussed the ordinal roots of mystery. I will now consider the origins of mystery in judgment and query. There are at least four pervasive modes of judgment, and it is important for mystery both that the modes are pervasive and that they are plural. In addition, there are novel forms of conjoint modality in judgment, perhaps even novel modes of judgment. I will discuss these three aspects of judgmental modality separately, to the extent that it is possible to do so, before considering query.

To say that there are plural modes of judgment is to say at least that there are plural modes of validation. This means that the mode of validation relevant to one mode of judgment is mysterious relative to another while at the same time subject to its conditions. The validation appropriate to a given mode of judgment is inexplicable as a mode of validation relative to the other modes of judgment, while it is amenable to judgment in all the modes. The combination of the two principles—plurality of validation conjoined with pervasiveness of judgment—entails that validation is always mysterious while remaining indefinitely open to further judgment.

For example, we may consider active or moral judgment from the standpoint of assertive judgment. Some moral philosophers have tried to assimilate active judgment to assertive judgment. It is possible to do so by postulating certain ideal ends which are not subject to criticism—outside query. Active judgment would then be the determination of the most effective means for attaining the postulated ends. An alternative is to regard active judgment as a form of inquiry seeking to establish general principles of successful action—entirely a substantive or hypothetical basis for action. An ideal here would be a generalization representing successful past actions extended hypothetically into novel situations. In the first approach, ideals are an intransigent mystery. In the second approach, obligation is equally intransigent. Action is not assertion; truth is not sufficient to establish successful action. Yet the conditions of action may be studied assertively in the social and behavioral sciences. Thus, active validation is incongruous with assertive validation, yet not closed to assertive query.

The converse is equally remarkable: that a supreme passion for truth is inexplicable from the standpoint of active judgment. Is truth morally advantageous in every case? From a political or moral point of view, an exclusive concern for truth is sometimes morally destructive. The truth may contribute to the good life, but particular scientific experiments may be harmful. Scientific research which leads to weapons of war is always morally problematical. A more compelling example is that of medical research into disease and therapy: the experimentation necessary to biology and medicine can never be morally neutral. Science is often immoral; morality is often assertively arbitrary. Scientific and moral validation are mysteries from the standpoint of the other, while each is subject to judgments from the other mode.

Constructive judgment is equally inexplicable from the standpoint of the other modes: art is often unconcerned with truth; and when of moral significance, its role is complex and difficult to delineate. Political concerns entail that art should serve the good life and be subordinated to action — though it would appear then to be less art; and it would seem impossible for art to defend claims to truth. From an artistic point of view, science is inhuman and uninteresting, routine and repetitive; life is too serious and too demanding. Active judgment seeks control to human ends; art may emphasize irony and detachment. Art is a mystery from the perspectives of science and morals; science and morals are mysterious from the standpoint of judgments whose aim is creation. To a person of great artistic sensitivity, the world is but a means to greater enhancement and imaginative construction — neither correspondence nor control.

Metaphysics and syndetic judgment are typically mysterious from the standpoint of all the other modes — and mysterious though comprehensiveness is an important aspect of every mode of query. Comprehensiveness in science is in the service of truth; in ethics in the service of control; in art a means to distinctiveness. But metaphysics and its unique mode of validation are mysterious from the standpoint of all the other modes. Metaphysics is not simply assertion, and goes beyond the available evidence, coordinating diverse orders in a created order of discourse akin to but not art. Metaphysics accommodates action as one of its coordinating constituents — but is not action itself (or is but one kind of action). Metaphysics is not art, for it is concerned with truth as art cannot be.

There are many modes of judgment and many modes of validation; and every mode is a mystery relative to the others. Novel modes of judgment may be created which are unions of the others: but they neither preempt the others nor abolish their uniqueness. Plurality in judgment is a permanent and inevitable source of mystery; yet every mystery is open to further consideration and judgment. The mysteries are everywhere; but they are not opaque, intransigent, or absolute.

(h) *Pervasive Modes of Judgment.* The principle that describes the pervasiveness of judgment is that every judgment belongs to every mode. Yet we cannot say without qualification that a mode of judgment is *all*-pervasive. There is no totality of things or judgments, not even a totality of experience. Judgment does not include sufficiently remote or trivial events and experiences — though what was once neglected may be judged in the future. There are human events and products which are not judgments; but when judged, they are located in all the modes at once, at least as potentialities for further judgment.

I have spoken of this pervasiveness of judgment in describing the plurality of modes of judgment. For insofar as there is such a plurality, judgments valid in one mode are mysterious from the standpoint of other modes. Now this would be unimportant except for the condition that a judgment valid in one mode is also a judgment in another mode and open to its mode of validation. The mystery is that a human product may play quite different roles in different modes of judgment. The condition is the analogue in judgment of the principle that every order has many integrities. This varying integrities of judgmental orders are the origin of profound and enduring mysteries.

The mystery is more complex than I have shown so far. Given an order open to judgment, whether trivial or important, a plurality of modes of judgment is relevant with differing modes of validation. What, then, is the *correct* way to judge any given event? For example, is it more correct to seek true assertions about the stars, to seek to reach them and gain control over them, to live different lives by means of them, or to write poetry to them? Given important human events — starvation and suffering: is it more correct to understand them, to control them, or to create works of art inspired by them? Every answer is ordinal. The pervasiveness of judgment supports a plurality of modes.

There are limits to none of the modes relative to the others, while they are collectively plural.

The pervasiveness of each mode of judgment entails that nothing in experience is located within a single mode. There is the mystery that many disparate modes of validation prevail, while there may be no means of unifying them. This is a permanent source of mystery in human life: the challenge to gain a unity in knowledge, inspired by the pervasiveness of the modes of judgment, conjoined with a permanent plurality in validation and judgment. The mystery is exacerbated by the fact that unification is frequently attainable: we often find or create novel unions of query and judgment. Yet unification is also frequently unattainable. When attained, it is always limited. In addition, constituent orders of a superaltern order may preserve their standards of validation relative to the inclusive system. There is a permanent tension between comprehensiveness and plurality, exacerbated by the pervasiveness of the modes of judgment.

(i) *Created Modes of Judgment.* Not only are there many and diverse modes of judgment: there are also possibilities for creating novel modes of judgment—at least novel methods and forms within an established mode and novel intermodal forms of query with novel modes of validation. Now assertive, active, and constructive judgment may be viewed as expressions of the pervasive functions of saying, doing, and making. and rooted in primordial natural conditions. Syndetic judgment would appear either to be engendered by query or rooted in a fourth pervasive function of unifying—expressed, for example, in the early religions.

In either case, the prospects for invention in judgment are clear. Given the pervasive functions of saying, doing, making, and unifying, there are diverse forms of query in which method is fused with validation. If the primordial form of unification is religion, it is radically transformed in philosophy. If we begin with the three pervasive functions of saying, making, and doing, syndetic judgment is created by intermodal query. We may note the intermodality of philosophy, history, the social sciences, religion, and art criticism. I should also mention new sub-sciences

109

such as biochemistry and chemical physics.

It is a difficult and complex issue whether history and the social sciences, even art criticism and interpretation, are to be associated with their own modes of judgment, or whether they are forms of query comprised of other modes. I have associated the notion of a mode of judgment with *pervasiveness*: a mode of judgment rests on a mode of validation applicable in principle to all judgments. Here the functions of saying, doing, and making are extremely important. Nevertheless, there is also syndetic judgment.

On the surface, a discipline such as art criticism does not have the pervasiveness of assertion or action; yet this is deceptive. Art criticism is, after all, the interpretation and evaluation of created works. To the extent that constructive judgment is pervasive throughout human experience, the evaluation and interpretation of constructed works is equally pervasive. No element of experience may be regarded as intrinsically irrelevant to constructive judgment or to the interpretation of works of art. Not only works of fine art, but works of design, created lives, created philosophic systems — the full range of constructive judgments — admit of complex articulation through all the modes of judgment: description, evaluation, interpretation, and comprehension. Any judgment may be of interpretive relevance in the context of constructive judgment.

The social sciences may also appear to be of limited pervasiveness. Sociology is explicitly distinguished from the psychological sciences, and if we take the larger category of the behavioral sciences, we seem to address individual behavior more than institutions. The union of the behavioral and social sciences with active judgment — the study of human relationships emphasizing control and action — has wide pervasiveness, but essentially as a mode of active judgment. Politics is the unifying activity that brings together the social and behavioral sciences with aspects of control through policy and action that is pervasive throughout human experience. Politics here is a dominant form of active judgment. On this view of things, the social sciences are a branch of active query, involving no unique modes of judgment. They may also be viewed as a branch of scientific query. Whether they represent a unique form of intermodal query emphasizing both assertive and active query has not been established. The more distinctive are the methods of the social sciences, and the more pervasively do they represent a way of understanding all aspects of human experience, the more legitimate is their claim to comprise a new and unique mode of judgment and query.

History seems clearly pervasive enough to mark a unique mode of judgment. Every human product belongs to time — though not exclusively to time. The number system does not have a history, for it has no temporal location: but its discovery and development has a history. Everything in human experience may be assigned temporal locations relative to its scope, if not its integrity. History, then, is all-pervasive in experience. Is it merely assertive judgment relative to time and experience? Or is it a unique union of active, assertive, comprehensive, and constructive judgment? If the latter, and historical explanation possesses a unique mode of validation, then historical judgment has been created in the course of human experience.

The question of whether a given form of query is the expression of a unique mode of judgment is difficult and controversial. I have delineated four modes of judgment. There may be many more. Far more important, novel modes of judgment may be engendered in the interplay of established modes. Plurality and pervasiveness together, while they cannot guarantee inventiveness, establish the permanent prospect of novel modes of judgment and query. We have seen in the last few hundred years the advance of first a few, then many physical sciences, the birth of the social sciences, art history, political economics, and so forth. There are new roles for governments to play, new modes of action and control, new conceptions of art. Intermodal forms of query are engendered by changing conditions of life and in the interplay of query in the diverse modes of judgment.

It follows that every subject matter is mysterious in the ways which novel modes of query afford — especially, that however completely an order is known within a certain mode of judgment, other possibilities, other modes, of knowledge remain.

The plurality of modes of judgment entails that there is no one or supreme way of knowing. The possibility of novel modes of query exacerbates this condition. As new methods of historical analysis are invented, the very nature of our understanding of the past changes. Nevertheless, newer modes of validation do not always supplant older modes; novel modes of judgment and query are mysterious from the standpoint of established modes, but the latter may be equally mysterious in return. The truth of myths is as alien to science as science is to early cosmologies.

(j) *Query.* The process in which novel modes of judgment are engendered is query. I have noted four of the forms of query, each of which emphasizes a mode of judgment: science, ethics, art, and metaphysics. The plurality of modes of judgment and their pervasiveness of scope admit a continuing possibility that novel modes of query may be engendered. Now environmental conditions of human life have a great impact on and sustain active judgment. Political and economic supports have effects encouraging or inhibiting inventiveness and originality. In addition, activities that do not explicitly belong to query may have intermodal impact—for example, novel forms of historical analysis may emerge from totalitarian political orders or communal religious practices. Nevertheless, the greatest source of novelty in judgment is query: the greatest responsibility of query is not validation but invention.

If so, then query is the greatest source of mystery. The world is obdurate and plural; we invent and pursue, to find our goals always eluding us, shifting with our activities and changing conditions. Query is the source of ongoing judgments and inventions; these change the world. Novel orders of great scope are engendered. Men change their instruments and their judgments. Query is the hallmark of the plurality of possibilities surrounding us—so that the more we know, the more we change in ourselves and our surroundings, producing further mysteries.

Query reflects the manipulative, transformative role of man as judge. The possibilities resident in orders of action make every deed precarious, engendering unforeseen and unforeseeable results. Successful query radically modifies its surroundings. In

112

this respect, query is indefinitely plural and open, both when it is inventive and even when it is successful in established ways. Mysteries are a consequence as well as a condition of successful query. I have come again to my central thesis: that mystery is not a sign of failure, incompetence, or absolute limitation, but is a manifestation of knowledge and the achievements of query.

However, before I offer a definition and analysis of mystery, and show that mystery pertains intrinsically and affirmatively to query, therefore to rationality and cognition, I must address several subsidiary matters. In particular, I must consider the importance and role of mystery not only in philosophy but in science, ethics, art, and the branches of philosophy other than metaphysics. If mystery is intrinsic to query, then the view that science overcomes mystery is false. I must also come to terms with the distinction between ultimate, intransigent mysteries and plural mysteries amenable to reason. Here too, if mystery pertains intrinsically to query, absolute and intransigent mysteries are unsupportable. My remaining discussions will show that mystery is a face of successful query and that query opens up prospects of mystery — entailing that knowledge is always mysterious while mystery is always knowable.

Mystery and Judgment

I have approached mystery through philosophy which confronts it directly and dwells among it as no other mode of query can. Wherever mysteries are considered directly in their enduring character we pass into the provinces of philosophy. Moreover, the syndetic function of philosophy brings before it all enduring mysteries of query. In order to counter the hypothesis that mystery pertains only to philosophy, I must briefly examine the mysteries which play a role in the major forms of knowledge: science, ethics, art, and philosophy itself.

(a) *Science.* It is commonly held that science eliminates mystery, not only by repudiating what is intransigently unknowable, but by its own successes. We may expect that to properly formulated scientific questions upon any subject whatsoever, there will be found scientific answers. The advances of science appear to dispel all mysteries.

The reply is that answers do not dispel mysteries. Mystery is prevalent in the plurality of orders and modes of judgment: it is found everywhere in human experience. What science does is to restrict itself to questions that can be given univalent answers— and there are such questions and answers throughout all domains of experience. We may understand such a form of query in terms of the integrity of orders. A correspondence may be established between an order of discourse and the integrity of another order, and by suitable restrictions and qualifications, the scope of the order and its possibilities may be rendered irrelevant. We may say that science addresses itself only to questions that can be given univalent answers. We may also say that science seeks maximal compulsion for its answers—defined again in terms of univalent validation. To the extent that there are questions which can be given such answers, science is enormously successful; it is also relatively unmysterious. It achieves its successes by determining ordinal perspectives in which univalence is attainable, in which integrities can be determined relatively precisely, in which mysteries are of minimal relevance.

But mystery cannot be eliminated. Science can legislate neither to events nor to other modes of query. If there are questions that can be given univalent answers relative to one mode of query, there are other questions and modes of query which afford no such answers. Mysteries remain in ethics, art, politics, and philosophy regardless of the successes of the sciences. Among the plural modes of judgment and query, there might be one devoid of mystery: but it would not eliminate mystery from the other modes. Suppose science addressed only questions with clear and definite answers: would this eliminate mystery? Or would it only show that certain mysteries can be ignored within suitable perspectives? Only a normative conviction that scientific explanation alone is legitimate, scientific judgment alone cognitive, can suggest that science might altogether eliminate mystery. Because there are many modes of query, science cannot eliminate mystery: it can at best ignore it.

114

But in fact science can do nothing of the sort. The great successes of science—univalent and precise achievements, profound and far-reaching theories—belong to the most general sciences. Astrophysics is science *par excellence*. Studies of the solar system are inconclusive by comparison, engendering many significant mysteries. Why are there nine planets rather than fourteen or three? Why are the planets located where they are? Were the asteroids a planet that disintegrated? Not only do we not know the answers to all such questions: the answers depend on local presuppositions about past circumstances whose specificity will always be partly indeterminate. There is a central mystery in science of the particular observations from which explanation proceeds. We can relate events by general laws, but each event remains mysterious in part, and so do the laws. There is a mystery to many events taken together when they comprise no single system of relations. There is always an element of coincidence, a consequence of a multiplicity of relevant determinations.

Many of the mysteries of being and knowledge apply directly to the sciences. Scientists may ignore certain mysteries—but they nevertheless remain. Science attains maximal determinateness, specificity, and compulsion in the context of mystery. It does so by emphasizing actualities and integrities rather than possibilities and scopes; but these are then always mysterious, There are always unforeseen possibilities, unexpected relevancies. The general laws of the physical sciences are applied in particular cases only with grave risks of error. In such applications, the mysteries of science are transformed into indeterminate possibilities for action, and we may deny that they belong to science. Yet they are engendered by scientific query, and they may be resolved—to the extent that resolution is possible—only through further scientific query (though not scientific query alone).

Science attains its maximal determinateness and univalence by means of context-determining assumptions—for example, that real gases behave like ideal gases, finite masses like point particles, and so forth; but most important, that certain systems are effectively closed. Now it is fundamental within the ordinal

115

theory that no order is closed, that possibilities prevail in all orders, that every order is interrelated with others and possesses many integrities and scopes. The tension between singular and plural integrities is a permanent source of mystery in science.

There are scientists (and philosophers) who believe that science purports to grasp the furdamental nature of the universe in which we live and to define it in all space and time. They believe that there is one universe, closed to explanation, and that knowledge will someday exhaust the universe, at least in all fundamental respects. Such scientists ignore the plurality of sciences and modes of judgment. They ignore ordinal plurality. They may be accused of seeking to eliminate mystery — but not simply as scientists, for their presuppositions are not esential to their scientific achievements.

(b) *Ethics.* If science cannot eliminate mystery, and does not purport to do so except in the limited sense defined, ethics surely cannot and does not try — though determinateness and control are of primary concern for active judgment. The most obvious mystery in action is that defined by Kierkegaard: no rational considerations can obliterate the gap between deliberation and action.

An obvious reply is that action is not deliberation: therefore, deliberation cannot be expected to determine action. We may, then, expand the mysteries of active judgment in two fundamental ways. First, because every act is specific and transpires in a context of plural possibilities, every act is perilous. No mode of action, under the most controlled forms of query, can avoid failure. We may take the risk of failure into account, and seek to do the best we can. Still, the central mystery of active judgment prevails in all political undertakings. In matters of importance, we are certain to fail in some respects, from some points of view. Failures are due not merely to intransigent circumstances, to obdurate conditions: they are also caused by the best intentions, by the effectiveness of rational powers, and by modifications of human expectations.

The second mystery is more striking, and the basis of all relativism. The difficulty with most forms of relativism is that

116

they do not consider the extent to which ideals and methods may be common among people of different characters and styles. The truth of relativism is that different agents in similar circumstances may perform different but equally valid actions. There is a plurality inherent in action that assertive judgment seeks to avoid: a plurality rooted in human differences and a fundamental diversity among interpretations of ideals. Common ideals pass into diverse forms of action, each mysterious from the standpoint of the others. The plurality of valid actions reflects the plurality of possibilities resident in every situation and the disparity of individual perspectives coordinated within a shared community.

(c) *Art*. In one sense, art may have no mysteries, for in general it may not seek understanding. Its knowledge — the result of artistic query — may be inherently intransitive. To know by art is to create: perfectly. inventively, distinctively. Constructive judgment may be said to have no mysteries for it seeks to give no answers — and there are mysteries only relative to questions and answers. Nevertheless, there are questions in the sense that there is query. There are also the questions which arise in other modes of judgment relative to art and constructive judgment.

Instead of saying that there is no mystery in art, for art seeks to dispel no mystery, we may say instead that art is *entirely* mysterious, the mystery of creation. Constructive judgment is the creation of novel orders emerging from past traditions yet departing from them. To the extent that we simply have a work of art, there is no mystery: merely the work. Nevertheless, the work has relations; it is perfect relative to other creations and orders; it is original relative to what is common and traditional; it is celebrative in contrast with what is ordinary. Its relations to other orders are essential to it, yet it is an idiosyncratic and sovereign creation. The relations of a work of art to other works, to its author's life, to the rest of human experience, even to its own constituents, are persistently mysterious. It is the mystery of how novelty and significance can be fashioned of established and commonplace materials.

(d) *Philosophy*. All the mysteries I have discussed are mysteries

117

of philosophy. Philosophy draws upon all the mysteries of query, interrogating and interweaving them in its syndetic role. Comprehensiveness is a permanent mystery where all-encompassment is impossible. Comprehensiveness also confronts the mystery of how what is separate and distinct may also be unified and related.

Philosophy comprises many activities and methods besides syndetic judgment. It is a permanent and interrogative union of the four modes of judgment, continually defining novel modes of analysis and synthesis. It continually seeks new starting points, confronting and rejecting all prior methods. Even where syndetic functions are subordinate, philosophy is intermodal and novel; even where philosophy is traditional, it continually seeks new forms and methods. Philosophy as a mode of query is filled with mystery. Its greatest mystery is that it continually redefines its modes of validation and methods of judgment, as if it has no secure foundation or identity. If science takes too much for granted, thereby attaining maximal determinateness in the compulsion of evidence, philosophy takes nothing for granted including its own legitimacy, and continually redefines itself enveloped in permanent mystery. Nevertheless, though everything in philosophy is mysterious, everything is also amenable to rational understanding, though in an indefinite number of ways. There are permanent and omnipresent mysteries, but none is intransigent, absolute.

Ultimate Mysteries

There are no ultimate mysteries. Rationality demands that all mysteries be permeable, dissolving into other mysteries. Our pluralistic ontology defines an indefinite plurality of mysteries, and there can be no order and no mode of judgment without its mysteries. Nevertheless, each mystery is penetrable, amenable to indefinite revelation. There are orders which are unknowable: no possibility prevails of knowing them. Yet such uncogniscibility is intrinsic neither to judgment nor orders, but is a function of specific circumstances of judgment and experience. An order

sufficiently remote from human experience is unknowable—
remote in time or space or lost unrecoverably. No possibility of its
judgment may prevail in any human perspective. This is no more
of an ultimate mystery than that an event might once have been
known by men yet lost in the recesses of time. There are orders
which are unknowable in present and future experience and
orders which are unknowable in all human experience due to its
ordinal conditions. But no order is intrinsically or in principle
unknowable.

We may again consider the great cosmological mysteries of
God and the world. The mystery of the world is that anything
prevails. Ordinality entails that there is no world, therefore no
mystery of its prevalence. There is also no ultimate mystery of
non-being, for not to be in one order is to be in another. Apart
from ordinality, the mystery of existence entails its own intransigence. There can be no final explanation for the world. Ordinality avoids the ultimacy and intransigence of this conclusion by
denying that there is a world to be given an explanation. Orders
are interrelated; we explain or understand one in terms of another,
and all explanations are ordinal. Moreover, all orders are located
somewhere. Even God prevails in certain orders. Yet if there is a
God, his relations may make him accessible to query. Mysteries
intrinsically inaccessible to query violate rationality and ordinality.

The common form taken by ultimate mysteries has been in
terms of the divine. And although religion, like philosophy and
science, may be a pervasive human activity, it may violate the
spirit of query in its concern for ultimate mystery. In postulating
ultimate mysteries, religion and theology close off aspects of
experience to query. Mystery passes over into intransigence;
rationality is abrogated.

The classic "problems" of philosophy are nearly always mysteries. Yet the history of philosophy forcibly demonstrates that
the great mysteries are not intransigent, but recurrently approach-
able. We may not be able to blend mind and body—but after all,
they are not exactly the same in all respects. Instead, they pose
a recurrent challenge to philosophical query to define their

119

relations while not dissipating their distinctness. As a mystery, the mind-body dualism is not ultimate but many-faceted, each facet indefinitely amenable to further query.

Ultimate mysteries define certain orders as intransigent and unrelated — at least, unmediatable relative to thought and query. Yet how might one prove that a given order is closed to query except by penetrating it somewhat? There may be orders which are both unrelated and unmediated. Yet they are either *entirely* disconnected, thus no mystery at all, for they are beyond the reach of judgment; or if they admit some relations with human experience, they are not entirely intransigent.

Were ultimate mysteries closed entirely to judgment, they would be unmentionable, unexaminable, unimaginable — *utter silence*. They would be nothing at all relative to human perspectives, not even mysterious. Far too often God and the cosmic universe are held open to judgment while closed to query. And this is self-contradictory, since wherever there is judgment there may be query.

The principle that ultimate and intransigent mysteries are indefensible and unintelligible is a criterion for judging a philosophical viewpoint: does it dissipate mysteries or install them in rigid permanence? There is the third alternative of denying mystery — but I have thoroughly disposed of that point of view. The principle mentioned may be defended in two ways. First, in terms of the theory of orders, a theory of ultimate mystery is simply wrong. It repudiates relatedness yet rests on a relational foundation. It is self-contradictory. Second, ultimate mysteries may be attacked in terms of query. For philosophy is a predominant mode of query, if not its purest spirit. And ultimate mysteries are antithetical to query. This is true not only of religious and divine mysteries, but of philosophical cosmologies and intransigent scepticisms. Orders are plurally open to judgment. There are many mysteries, but they are intrinsically and indefinitely plural; and none is ultimate.

The Nature of Mystery

Mysteries are plural: they prevail at every boundary of judgment. We may therefore regard mystery as a face of judgment, reflecting the openness of orders to query. It does not hide the world from us, but is implicit in the effectiveness of judgment and its powers. The more effective the powers of the mind, the more pressing and diverse are the mysteries which confront us.

My immediate concern is not with the positive aspect of mystery, but with its nature. I have traced its origins to ordinality. Every order is inexhaustible in its locations and integrities; every judgment is inexhaustible in the same respects, thus disparate in its integrities and ramifications. There is a disparity between the integrities of orders of judgment and the integrities of other orders, inevitable where perfect identity is lacking. There is disparity among the integrities of every order, inevitable because of ordinal plurality. These disparities issue in mystery.

What is the nature of mystery? Can we formulate an answer in sufficiently general terms to apply to all modes of judgment and query, as well as to the diverse perspectives in which judgment takes place? As I have noted, orders outside experience and judgment may be plural and diverse, complex in their interrelations. Yet they are not as such mysterious. Mystery is a condition of judgment, produced by judgment, though it is not a function of judgment alone. The plurality and diversity of orders is the *pre*condition of mystery. Ordinality establishes the general basis for mystery. But mysteries belong only to query. Unless there is a relevant question, there can be no mystery. Unless the questions are persistent, mystery is obscured. God is no mystery in the absence of interrogation and judgment: he prevails silently. I have rejected absolute and intransigent mysteries for many reasons, one of which is that in being absolute, such mysteries violate query. They are not then mysteries, but surds.

Mystery pertains intrinsically to query. It is the residue that obtains in the context of successful query—the questions that remain unanswered where answers have been forthcoming. It is, then, the indeterminateness inherent in ordinality—qualified by

121

determinateness, functionality, and complementarity—brought into and definitive of query. I have defined query as interrogative judgment for its own sake, methodic interrogation through the diverse modes of judgment. Every judgment is mysterious in that the questions we can ask can never be given completely satisfactory answers. The most penetrating answers engender the most profound of novel questions. This condition can be given a positive and a negative cast. Sceptically, we may say that all knowledge is limited, that no answer is sufficient. The plurality of orders entails that judgment can only attain partial and relative validation. Scepticism is a natural consequence of ordinality, and mystery may be regarded entirely in terms of the limitations of knowledge.

However, from the standpoint of query and ordinality, mystery has a far more constructive interpretation. What seems implicit in the sceptical point of view is an absolute standard of knowledge—either the world as a whole or the thing in itself. Ordinality dismisses both the world as a whole and the thing in itself. One consequence may be a greater scepticism, for we may demand an absolute perspective as a condition of knowledge. The alternative is to accept query and its valid fruits, however ordinal, as the basis of all knowledge. Here mystery is not an expression of the limits of knowledge, but of its attainments within query. Query is perpetual interrogation, ongoing judgment. Were there complete and final knowledge to be attained, query could prevail no longer. It would have no further mystery. Not only is this absurd from the standpoint of ordinality and inexhaustibility: it is self-contradictory that there might be a mode of knowledge that could supercede query where query is the basis of knowledge.

Mystery expresses the fact that query always possesses additional possibilities, that there are always further questions, novel judgments, additional considerations. No judgment can answer all relevant questions or attain validation for all times and places, all perspectives. Validation is ordinal, and ordinality entails a permanent diversity and prospect for query. In this respect, mystery is the face of ordinality relative to query. It is the continuing possibility of further query, involving novel concerns and realizations. It is also the intrinsic limitation of every query, its incompleteness and ordinality.

Mystery is equivalent with ordinal possibility and plurality in judgment. Nevertheless, a distinction between two kinds of mystery is of fundamental importance. The prospects of query may have a heterogeneous or diverse quality: questions and answers giving way indefinitely to other questions and other answers. The unremitting character of query may take form in some perspectives as an unconfined sequence of judgments of diverse character. Here query involves us continually in new questions and judgments, and mystery is essentially plural and heterogenous: the continual movement of a query which is never entirely satisfied, never entirely fulfilled.

By way of contrast, there are clusters of mysteries which revolve around each other—questions which are never fully resolved by the proposed answers. Many mysteries that emerge in a given perspective may remain with us indefinitely by possessing a common or continuing integrity—an identity relative to a superaltern order of time and query. Here we may say that many mysteries are really one; many questions are different forms of the same question. Mystery is still plural in two fundamental respects: there are many such clusters of mysteries; in addition, each cluster—each gross mystery—is comprised of indefinitely many and diverse subaltern mysteries.

We may distinguish the two modes of mystery in terms of ordinal categories. There are plural and diverse mysteries which possess no common integrity relative to a superaltern order: *deviant mysteries.* But there are also mysteries which comprise gross identities in the context of ongoing query: which prevail throughout query. A particular mystery may take an indefinite number of forms—for example, the mystery of the one and the many. Grossly speaking, relations, identity, the unity of the world, and ordinality are all different approaches to the same mystery which endures despite (and because of) the various approaches we take to it. There are philosophical mysteries that seem permanent, not in being intransigent and impenetrable, absolute mysteries, but to the contrary, in being continually open to reason and query, yet whose residual difficulties possess an ongoing, integral nature.

The distinction between the two kinds of mystery can be formulated in another way. Query is pervaded by a continual mystery of unending questions and unsatisfied judgments. This we may call the primordial mystery of query, the mystery of reason. All such mysteries may be regarded grossly as one and characterized as the mystery of ordinality realized in ongoing query. Mysteries of this nature are all the same simply as mysteries. But in addition, certain mysteries inherent in philosophical query form persistent clusters with specific gross integrities. There are mysteries which are rationally penetrable, indefinitely open to judgment and query, but which partake of common and enduring functional difficulties manifested through a wealth of different forms and manifestations. The ongoing challenge of query is to transform one mystery into another. Nevertheless, there are mysteries which change their form but not their nature—not their gross integrity relative to philosophical query generally. To many people, only these mysteries are truly mysterious: a residue within philosophical query of a gross and persistent integrity. It is not intransigent or absolute; but it is persistent while being thoroughly penetrable and changeable.

Reason and Mystery

If mystery and query are intimately related as I have suggested they are, then mystery and rationality are not opposed but are factors within a single process. Knowledge and mystery are mutually involved and mutually intelligible. The two central kinds of mystery are intrinsic to knowledge, not as limitations or final absolutes, but reflecting the permanent prospect of expanded query. The first sense of mystery, which I have called "primordial," is the dimension of query that poses permanent and novel prospects of interrogation. It would not be amiss to identify this with the permanent challenge of query, the permanent impulse inherent in knowledge as an activity rather than a result.

Primordial mystery is the condition of query that differentiates it from absolute standards of cognition. There is no absolute knowledge in the sense that there is nothing "in itself" to be known finally, and there is no world-perspective from whose standpoint absolute validation may be achieved. All knowledge is ordinal — relative to superaltern orders. Primordial mystery is the expression in judgment and query of ordinality in its full range of properties and qualifications. Relative to judgment and query, the mystery is that no judgment is valid without qualification. All validation is ordinal; therefore, there are always further possibilities of query, further questions that remain for judgment. Primordial mystery is a direct outcome of the condition that there are possibilities prevalent in every order, therefore that there are possibilities requiring further judgment in every order of judgment. It follows that primordial mysteries are most felicitously regarded as variable, unspecific, continually transformed into novel forms and questions. Nevertheless, primordial mystery may also be regarded as an enduring condition of query, a single mystery pervading all forms of knowledge: the mystery that there is always more to be learned, more room for further query, that there are limits and qualifications to all knowledge and query. The paradox of learning finds its resolution in the condition of primordial mystery: there is no unqualified knowledge, no judgment valid without qualification. It follows that we can only learn what we can and that there is always more to be learned. Conversely, however, orders and judgments are relational and complex, involving other judgments and orders indefinitely. It follows that the judgments and orders with which we are acquainted are constitutively relevant to other orders, and may make effective query possible in relation to them.

The second form of mystery is specific in the sense that a particular mystery can possess an enduring and relatively limited identity — if not permanent, an identity throughout different times, conditions, circumstances, and approaches. The distinction between specific and primordial mystery is useful in distinguishing scientific from philosophical mysteries. Science endeavors to dissipate mysteries into other mysteries — though it is faced with the permanence of primordial mystery. Philosophical mysteries are more specific, reflecting the condition that query, while it transforms the integrities of prevailing mysteries, nevertheless establishes functional relationships among them. The syndetic function of philosophy is manifested through the enduring and common mysteries that pervade philosophy. Ordinality entails that a specific mystery will have many forms and, in many fundamental respects (relative to differing philosophical methods, approaches, and superaltern orders), is comprised of many quite different mysteries. But where there is continuity or functional identity among many such diverse orders relative to a larger prevailing philosophical tradition, we may say the mystery is one in certain important respects. Most of the mysteries I have discussed are specific and enduring in the sense described here.

Now in what sense is specific mystery a limitation, a defect in query? There is the fact that a specific mystery continually recurs, apparently uneliminable. But primordial mystery is also unavoidable, though it changes its forms. Is there a greater power in query where one mystery is replaced by another *ad infinitum* through valid judgments than were a single mystery is given novel forms *ad infinitum?* Any preference here seems arbitrary. In neither case can we know everything, either in general or about anything in particular: a consequence of ordinality. Nor can any outcome of query be considered entirely settled. Nevertheless, valid judgments are available in both forms of query and pertinent to both kinds of mystery. Where valid judgments prevail, we cannot speak sceptically of limits of knowledge except relative to a world order, though there is none. Mystery is not a limitation or defect of reason, but a permanent challenge, though it takes two major forms. The emphasis in philosophy on syndetic judgment is manifested predominantly in the form of specific enduring mysteries. The emphasis in science on assertive judgment is manifested predominantly in the form of primordial mysteries given indefinitely many forms. The pervasiveness of both forms of judgment entails that both philosophy and science must always possess both forms of mystery.

Far more important, specific mysteries prevail in the sense

that a given integrity is common over a range of subaltern orders. In this sense, mysteries prevail throughout philosophic query in virtue of the methods and aims of philosophy. But every prevalence is deviant somewhere: from some standpoint, alien perhaps to the philosophic temper, where syndetic judgment is subordinate, every mystery can be dissolved into others. Conversely, every deviant mystery prevails somewhere: from some standpoint, where comprehensiveness is predominant, no problem is ever fully resolved. Here philosophy maintains the prevalence of enduring mysteries; science transforms mysteries indefinitely into others. But throughout the transformation of mysteries into various forms, the mysteries of rationality, intelligibility, ordinality, and inexhaustibility prevail. Likewise, every philosophical mystery that maintains its integrity through time is given a wealth of different forms and approached from a variety of different perspectives, each of which dissolves the mystery at least in certain respects.

The intimate relations of query and mystery, conjoined with the identification of rationality and query, entail that mystery is not a limitation of reason but one of its primary exemplifications. Only in the absence of query could there be no mystery. Mystery does not represent the failure of query, its intrinsic impotence, but the contrary: the power of query is to evoke mystery in one or both of its forms. Specific mystery appears to confine reason to the extent that the enduring mystery is unresolvable. But this is an error: specific mysteries are not closed to resolution but are penetrable and interrogable. The resolution does not eliminate the enduring character of the mystery. It does, however, transform it through query. A specific mystery endures because of and in the manifold forms given to it by successful query. Indeed, mysteries would fade away and be forgotten were they not maintained by unceasing query. Mystery is then the expression of rationality in its greatest powers.

Conversely, to deny mystery is to deny rationality. Rationality is commitment to mystery—understood in the two dimensions of interrogative persistence and interrogative challenge. Where there is no mystery, there can be no query, for query is ongoing interrogative judgment for its own sake. Ordinality entails that any question can belong to all the modes of judgment. Therefore, a judgment valid in one context will be open, unsatisfied, even invalid in other orders of judgment. Ordinality, intrinsic to rationality, entails mystery. Rational methods under the conditions of ordinality and inexhaustibility entail the acceptance of mystery.

Reason demands the acceptance of mystery in its two forms. There is the affirmation of mystery as a permanent challenge to further judgment. This is primordial mystery which I have associated with the moving spirit of query. It is a permanent feature of both active and constructive judgment, commonly acknowledged in action and art. A rational agent, in active judgment, must confront the omnipresence of failure at every turn. There are always uncontrolled possibilities. Rationality in art is creation in the context of alternative creations, the interplay of imaginative possibilities. Constructive judgment is a reveling in possibilities and a revelation of mystery in its primordial conditions. Every created work of art, especially in a novel genre or style, engenders novel possibilities for constructive judgment.

Assertive judgment seems not to affirm mystery so much as to be plagued by it. Yet even here, rationality entails that orders be indefinitely open to rational interrogation. Suppose there were a sentence which represented precisely the constituents of a given order. The sentence must be interpreted and validated; these involve other orders. Query is ongoing judgment: validation always looks to further judgment if not always to further query. Where query is absent, we have judgment whose restrictions and limitations have neither been defined nor assimilated. As judgment, assertion is ongoing, interminable, and its incompleteness is manifested in mystery.

We arrive at my final argument: that there can be no knowledge without mystery. Mystery is not the limit of knowledge but its spirit. Here we need look only at the nature of validation in the context of judgment. Without plural possibilities available to reason, coming to know would be impossible, query would be unintelligible. There could be no query without the ongoing mystery of relevant possibilities and relevant deviances. There could be no knowledge (as an activity) without ordinality and possibility, deviance and scope. In order for reason to penetrate to the nature of things, orders must be open to penetration — related and ordinal; and there must be possibilities of conformation and transformation. Were there no mysteries, there could be no query.

Prima facie, knowledge and query depend only on primordial mysteries — those which disintegrate into others without end. Yet as I have noted, where there are many and diverse mysteries, passing into each other indefinitely, there may be a perspective relative to which they possess a gross integrity. Not all mysteries can be coordinated into one comprehensive, fundamental, and therefore intransigent mystery. That would entail a world order. Nevertheless, deviant mysteries prevail in some order — and conversely, every enduring mystery may be regarded as a plurality of related but essentially heterogeneous mysteries. Even more important, where there are diverse orders with diverse integrities, we seek their unification in syndetic judgment. We return to philosophy and its unique role and importance in query. Specific mysteries are intrinsic to philosophy, especially to metaphysics, due to the relevance and character of syndetic judgment. Comprehensiveness is sought everywhere in philosophy; and one result of such generality is that what would otherwise be mere diversity is transformed into unified identity. The fundamental source of specific and enduring mysteries, which are a plurality of related questions with a common integrity, is the creation of comprehensive orders in which they are all constituents, to which they are all relevant. Where syndetic judgment is of primary significance, specific mysteries are common and unavoidable, a consequence of a generality which transforms a plurality of distinct mysteries into a single mystery manifested in a wealth of diverse forms. History has an intrinsically syndetic role; and there are branches of science — theoretical and cosmological — which are fundamentally syndetic. We therefore find specific and enduring mysteries in both history and science, as well as

129

in all the major forms of query. But all such mysteries pass into philosophy as a consequence of the importance of syndetic judgment to philosophic query.

VI.

IMPLICATIONS AND CONCLUSIONS

The theory of mystery is a part of the theory of query, with emphasis upon the endurance of questions and the incompleteness of answers. Query transforms the mysteries of reason, integrally or scopically, but cannot eliminate them. All mysteries may be viewed as one, under a comprehensive or gross integrity. All mysteries may be viewed as many, constantly changing their nature and significance. In the same sense, all knowledge may be viewed as one, grounded in the mysteries of reason and ordinality, or as indefinitely diverse, with a wealth of questions and answers, taking an indefinite variety of forms and based on an indefinite wealth of unifying principles.

It follows that the implications of mystery are important for all branches of knowledge and all forms of action, not for philosophy alone—though philosophy may concern itself more directly and explicitly with the mysterious side of query. The major implications, the central conclusions, of the theory of mystery are relevant fundamentally to every form of query, especially where the effectiveness of query and its outcomes are most prominent in our considerations. Even here, however, these implications may take many different forms. The central implications of the theory of mystery may be viewed as one, a continuing consequence of an enduring mystery; or they may be viewed as many, an indefinite range of implications to be expressed in an indefinite variety of forms.

There is an indefinite number of forms and kinds of mystery, some of which have been considered here; and they may be conjoined under a common heading of general mystery as readily as they may be differentiated into a host of varied and unresolved issues. There is, then, a fundamental and pervasive mystery at the heart of mystery: the mystery of the indeterminateness of mystery. In this sense, there is indeterminateness at the foundation of every determination of what is mysterious, and arbitrariness to every expression of mystery. Every society, every culture, expresses its own relationship to mystery in its own terms—subject, of course, to historical, social, and cultural determinants. There is no universal form of the expression of mystery, for there is no fundamental and supreme mystery. And there is no unconditioned form of the expression of mystery, for every expression is grounded in human and social conditions. These two conclusions follow from the two dimensions of the origin of mystery: the inexhaustibility of orders and the inexhaustibility of query.

However, certain expressions of the nature of mystery appear to be of fundamental importance to our time. One of these addresses the question of the finiteness of the universe, the completeness of our knowledge of it. Can we expect to attain completeness in any branch or sub-branch of science—if not in astrophysics, due to the enormous magnitude of the spatiotemporal universe, then in microbiology, geology, quantum mechanics? On a single, unqualified model of correspondence between our forms of expression and the integrity of things, incompleteness is a function of complexity and magnitude alone, and prospects of completeness are plausible, even probable. Only limitations of time and space will prevent our exhausting the nature of things.

The theory of mystery entails that query can never be complete, in principle as well as in practice. Incompleteness is a function not of the magnitude of orders but of their inexhaustibility—and of the corresponding inexhaustibility of judgment and query. As recurrently emphasized by Hegel and Dewey, query changes the world, and a field of science brought to completion in certain respects always engenders expanding prospects for understanding in other respects. Orders known through successful query have their scope if not their integrity transformed—manifested in the indefinite and inexhaustible transformations of mysteries realized by ongoing query. Knowledge of genetic structure opens unresolved questions of genetic control; knowledge of nuclear physics opens questions of nuclear energy and dangers of proliferation; knowledge of the causes of weather opens questions of the control of rainfall. Knowledge given by technology raises questions of the control of technology, but also of the very nature of technology and our subordination to its powers. Knowledge of the integrity of an order always expands its scope, confronting us with additional and undetermined considerations. Even more important, as the scope expands through cognitive control, new integrities are engendered. The greater our knowledge of the solar system, the greater the probability of life in space and the greater the wealth of new technological and social problems requiring resolution.

The social sciences absorb many of the transformations produced by scientific query and technology—and that is one of the important sources of their indeterminateness. The greater our knowledge of and control over the physical world, the more complex become the implications for social control and social institutions. Industrial technology manifests enormously sophisticated means of understanding and control, but almost always engenders more complex difficulties for control that it resolves. We may then say that science in its purest form involves minimal intervention in events from the standpoint of human control, but becomes a social institution—technology and engineering—where intervention and control are emphasized. Nevertheless, even the purest science intervenes in events and transforms the integrities of what it studies, either at the subatomic level or at a macroscopic level where experimentation always leaves recoverable traces. At certain stages of development, the study of Mars and the technological exploitation of its resources are indistinguishable.

The largest question concerning science (and technology) is not of controlling the outcomes of scientific query, but of the broad implications of such query. The question, in its simplest form, is "Why Science?" Yet in this form it suggests unreason and obscurantism, as if there were an alternative to scientific development, an alternative but rational avenue to knowledge of the physical world. From the standpoint of the theory of query, however, the question is fundamentally rational, for it addresses the nature and values of science from the standpoint of other perspectives, other modes of query, and is based on the intermodality of judgment and query. The most obvious—perhaps the most important—standpoint is one of action and control: shall we be subject to science or bring it under our control? Is technology an instrument or a social force? Of course, from the standpoint of an ordinal theory, controlling science and being influenced by it are not opposed but are complementarily and reciprocally related. Technology is both an instrument and a social force. More plausibly and modestly, is there a point of diminishing returns where sacrifices to scientific achievement are no longer repaid by adequate returns, where technology warps the quality of life more than it improves it, and so forth?

But these are relatively modest questions of limited scope, relative to alternative questions of the foundations of science and query. The question "Why Science?" may be given a more radical, extreme interpretation. Unfortunately, most expressions of the radical and far-reaching thesis tend toward obscurantism and uncontrolled relativism. We note that science has a social as well as an epistemic character: indeed, if scientific activities are to succeed, their social character must be as prominent as their confirmational or theoretical character. Here, then, science functions as one of many social institutions, competing politically and economically for resources and support. Here the power of science and technology is measured by social outcomes and the transformation of social forms, not by experiments carried out and theories constructed. As a consequence, from a radical enough perspective, emphasizing a sociological or anthropological point of view, the accomplishments of science are simply another expression of the contemporary forms of social organization.

Alternatively, we note that scientific query is fundamentally linguistic as well as historical, and that a science without language is unknown to us, perhaps unintelligible. But every language develops historically from prior languages. Every system develops from prior systems and is influenced profoundly by them. There is no perfect, pure language, none untarnished by the arbitrariness of earlier forms. There are no theories without presuppositions, no languages without preconditions. Every expression, however grounded in experiment and theory, is derived from an arbitrary and irrelevant historical background: English rather than Sanskrit, Latin roots rather than Egyptian, metric units rather than British units, and so forth.

In both cases, the conclusion is that there can be no form of scientific query, no form of assertive judgment, that is *entirely* grounded in evidence. In terms of the theory of mystery, no form of query and validation can be assertive judgment alone and brought under assertive validation alone. All judgment and query are multi-modal; all orders are multi-ordinal and multi-integral. Mystery is a consequence of the plurality of orders and of modes of judgment. Expressed in yet another way, mystery is a function of the forms of indeterminateness that complement the modes of determinateness in rational undertakings. Determinateness and indeterminateness are complementary and all-pervasive: possibility with actuality; scope with integrity; integrities with every gross integrity; deviance with prevalence; and so forth:—but also, social and moral forms of assertive query; constructive and aesthetic considerations in theoretical analysis; a human context for all query, even where addressing the entirely inorganic and remote recesses of the spatiotemporal universe.

These considerations, in the context of a non-mysterious paradigm of science, generate scepticism, even despair. The theory of mystery provides us with a very different perspective on the diverse considerations: that indeterminateness is a component of all forms of determinateness; that query is therefore unending and interminable, constantly changing its forms and achievements. The scepticism is avoided by the realization that mystery is the indeterminateness that makes discovery possible, that questions depend on plurality and indeterminateness while answers depend on questions. The functionalism of the theory of orders entails that every answer is ordinal, dependent on

135

conditions and circumstances. Nevertheless, the validation of query for a particular perspective, if functional, is not arbitrary, and there are wider as well as narrower perspectives, including perspectives men share in common.

We live in a time in which a scientific model of rationality has become predominant. But it is a limited and partial model, limited relative to the social and human sciences by presuppositions drawn from the physical sciences, and limited as well relative to the many other forms of query. A reaction against the excesses of such a model is then emergent, rooted in social and psychological considerations and concerns about the foundations of language and thought. The most serious limitation of the model, however, is too seldom confronted: that it is *monolithic*, but a single model of query imposed on a wealth of forms of conception and cognition. The alternatives suggest to many philosophers that other equally monolithic systems should prevail: the historical or social approach to explanation, the grounding of rationality in the conditions of human life.

In the rare cases where plurality is acknowledged and understood, and social, historical, as well as physical considerations are seen to be complexly interrelated, the absence of a dominant explanatory perspective suggests extreme scepticism. The theory of orders, with the associated theories of mystery and query, provides a resolution of this difficulty—though not a resolution without its mysteries, not a resolution satisfactory in all respects. Nevertheless, the ordinal and perspectival basis of validation and query entails a pluralistic and heterogeneous theory of rationality, dependent finally on the intermodal forms of query, which are themselves diverse and heterogeneous. Validated query is accepted as authoritative, but with its limits and indeterminacies as well as its compulsions and necessities.

Here, then, mystery pervades all query: but it is neither incompatible with validation nor ultimately sceptical, but expressive of the incomplete, ongoing character of query. The demand mystery imposes on query is for additional query, unending. But it does not do so by scepticism or rejection, but in terms of the very power and authority valid query brings.

All the forms of query, then, with continual prospects of new forms, comprise the pluralistic and heterogeneous arena of rational activities, reducing to no single authoritative perspective and grounded in no supreme monolithic vision of human life. Here no single perspective on human experience or the world is acceptable — neither economic nor chemical, biological nor physical, mechanical nor purposive, scientific nor philosophical. Instead, the mysteries of every form of query are viewed as accomplishments and limitations simultaneously, calling for the continual invention of new approaches which broach modal boundaries, and for the continual development of new modes of validation in established modes of query. Here science brings enormous epistemic authority, but neither a complete nor final authority, and by no means one without fundamental and pervasive mysteries. Here only additional query can resolve the mysteries engendered by query — but query in all its forms and modes, including new forms yet to be invented.

The theory of mystery and of ordinal judgment and query entails the inexhaustibility of orders and the inexhaustibility of query — including scientific query. But its implications for science are only one way of construing its importance and relevance, a way particularly significant in a scientific age. As I have noted, the inexhaustibility of mystery entails an inexhaustibility of consequences and implications, for philosophy and for all branches of knowledge. We may consider, then, another general expression of the nature of mystery of particular relevance to contemporary experience. This is more general than that given above concerned with scientific query, for it considers human life in a more general perspective. It replaces the older modes of expression grounded in God and religion that presuppose more about the natural, supernatural, and human orders than we are willing to grant today. It suffers, as it must, from alternative presuppositions which we may not all be willing to grant, and which may well be rejected under different cultural conditions. A major factor underlying its relevance is the combined growth of the social and human sciences, with the sense of social and political inadequacy that prosperity has brought, a pessimistic sense of human achievement conjoined with the greatest means of power and control that man has ever had.

The mystery is expressed in the general question: "What are the possibilities for human life?" Its limitations are apparent: it locates mystery in judgment and action, overlooking the mysteries of natural order. It looks for indeterminateness in human affairs, overlooking the wealth of indeterminants in the plurality of orders and their interrelations. It emphasizes human possibilities—and their limits—while possibilities are relevant to all orders. By neglect, it appears to presuppose a determinate order of natural events rendered indeterminate and ambiguous only in human terms.

Yet the question and its associated mysteries are remarkably powerful, and can be construed in productive ways that express a staggering wealth of mysteries relevant to contemporary society. The possibilities for human life are, of course, alternatives in human understanding and action. Technically speaking, according to the theory of orders, possibilities are always relevant to particular perspectives and orders. The question, as it stands, is therefore unrestricted, unqualified, and suffers from obscurity and unintelligibility. There are alternative possibilities of political order other than those realized, but it is unintelligible to speak of possibilities of orders grounded in no actual circumstances or conditions.

Nevertheless, the question points to the conditions which underlie every determination, the further conditions that underlie those conditions, and so forth; the indeterminants that are relevant *ad infinitum* to every determination. In other words, it points to the pervasiveness of mystery as a joint function of determinateness and indeterminateness, actuality and possibility. It may be construed as a question about time and the future, as Hegel and Marx construe it: possibilities for the future. And in this sense, it is severely limited and of only modest application, though of no less importance for its limitations. Alternatively, however, it may be construed as a question about possibilities in every sphere of human life: possibilities resident in every judgmental context. Now even in this sense, it manifests a limited sense of indeterminateness. There are deviances, scopes, and plural integrities relevant to every order as well as possibilities and actualities. Still, the concept of possibility emphasizes the plural interrelations among orders, the multiple modes of determination relevant to every order, and the indeterminateness fostered by such plurality. In this respect, it overlaps to a great extent with the other modes of plurality and indeterminateness, thereby implicating, if only indirectly, multiple integrities, deviances, and scopes.

The question, then, of the possibilities for human life, is of what is determinate insofar as we are natural creatures—biological and material—in an established social environment; but also, what is not determined by these conditions, and what would be indeterminate in other conditions, *ad infinitum.* The question is, in a way, an implied assertion: of the mysteriousness and indeterminateness inherent in all conditions, of the incompleteness of all query relevant to these conditions. In other words, the theory of mystery is the only full and rational answer to what is implied by the question—and an answer that cannot in principle be complete. Mystery haunts query. But it also is the foundation of query. As we engage in rational activities, bringing them to determinate fruition, we must be aware of the conditions that make them determinate and the implied alternatives within them. In this sense, mystery establishes the basis for query, its successes and its incompletenesses.

Here we see that the very achievements of the sciences—including their technological applications—manifest an urgent question of alternative possibilities: the sacrifices paid for scientific progress, the alternative cultural forms of development based on diminished technological capabilities. As I have put it, intermodal query leads us to the question of how beautiful and valuable is science, how politically effective and useful. Yet these questions are only of limited force unless we can also consider alternative prospects of scientific development, what science might be other than it is, how there might be cultural developments with a different way of utilizing technology. Note that we are not forced by reason to *undo* science and its technological

139

applications: we are not forced into an irrationalist position. Rather, we are asked only to understand the historical and social conditions that establish a basis for scientific and technological development and to criticize them in the light of imagined alternatives which we must also seek to understand and criticize.

Analogously, reason and query lead us to consider the determinants of political and social order—and of disorder as well. Such considerations inevitably entail a consideration of what is not so determined: what is capricious and arbitrary from the standpoint of our present social conditions. Social and political order are an outcome of controls exercised in active judgment, if not always purposive and methodic query, but also establish their own norms. Social institutions foster their own standards, however rooted they may have been in other, perhaps individualistic, norms when initiated. One of the problems for Western politics is the tradition of individualistic and liberal rhetoric, which tends to ignore the institutions which dominate contemporary human life that have established collectivistic standards. Politics is always collectivist in part, since its means are institutional and public. Once a plurality of norms and ends is engendered, resolutions become both inexhaustibly complex and mysterious. Political judgment is replete with mystery and indeterminateness, and no theoretical considerations alone can entirely resolve the complexity of political decisions in a complex and changing world.

The indeterminateness and complexity of political life do not entail expediency or lack of principle. To the contrary, only ideals and strongly-held principles can establish a basis for rational decisions and determinate actions. It is apparent, however, that the strength of our principles and ideals is not accompanied by simplicity and resolution in arriving at responsible courses of action in a complex world. Here again, the theory of mystery forcibly manifests the indeterminateness and incompleteness of all rational query in the context of the complexities of contemporary life. And it compels us to avoid dogmatic and thoughtless solutions where they manifest a disregard for alternative possibilities and courses of development.

140

Finally, like philosophy, contemporary art confronts the plurality of possibilities and mysteries directly, in its wealth of inventions and in the diverse ways in which we confront them. Contemporary art sometimes appears devoid of standards; and our interpretations and readings often appear arbitrary and relativistic. There is a concession to indeterminateness that distorts the character of mystery, transforming it into arbitrariness and incoherence, effectively abolishing its relationship to the conditions that provide determinateness. The theory of mystery is a theory of the conditions of judgments and orders, and is grounded in the complementary and inexhaustible relationship of determinateness and indeterminateness. No field besides philosophy so completely manifests the interplay of determinateness and indeterminateness, and revels in a wealth of deviant possibilities, as do the arts. But they sometimes seem to lapse into a total concession to indeterminateness, transforming mystery into arbitrariness and obscurity.

The theory of mystery, grounded in the theory of orders and of query, establishes a rational and intelligible foundation on which we may reexamine the conditions of human experience in their wealth of complexity in terms of what has been determined by past conditions and what might have been determined differently. The inexhaustibility of orders and of query entails that mysteries are ubiquitous and all-pervasive, and that the very conditions of life that promote determinateness engender new possibilities of understanding and action, producing new conditions in which determinateness and indeterminateness interact in new ways and new mysteries emerge and prevail. The intermodality of query is both a resolution of this process and an outcome inspired by it, grounded in an inexhaustible multiplicity of modes of determination. In final terms, mystery and inexhaustibility in query are the same: a revelation of the complexity inherent in the ordinal nature of every determination.

141

NOTES

Preface

1. See my *Transition to an Ordinal Metaphysics,* Albany, State University of New York Press, 1980. The theory of orders was first developed in Justus Buchler's *Metaphysics of Natural Complexes,* New York, Columbia University press, 1966; the theory of judgment and query was first delineated in Buchler's *Toward a General Theory of Human Judgment,* New York, Columbia University press, 1951, and *Nature and Judgment,* New York, Columbia University Press, 1955.

2. Ludwig Wittgenstein: *Tractatus Logico-philosophicus,* London, Routledge and Kegan Paul, 1961; Martin Heidegger: *Identity and Difference,* New York, Harper & Row, 1969; John Wisdom: "Metaphysics and Verification," *Mind,* XLVII, 1938, and other papers in *Philosophy and Psychoanalysis,* New York, Philosophical Library, 1953.

Introduction

1. Alfred North Whitehead: *Modes of Thought,* New York, Macmillan, 1938, p. 66.

2. Justus Buchler: *Toward a General Theory of Human Judgment,* pp. 121-22.

I. Being

1. Martin Heidegger: *Introduction to Metaphysics,* New Haven, Yale University Press, 1959, p. 14.

2. Martin Heidegger: "What is Metaphysics?," *Existence and Being,* Chicago, Regnery, 1949, p. 330.

3. The principle that the universe cannot be regarded collectively is essential to the ordinal theory. (See below, pp. 83-86.) It has a long history, ranging from Aristotle's discussions of Parmenides through Hume's *Dialogues on Natural Religion* and Dewey's and James's pluralism. (See following passages in text.) Detailed discussions of the essential plurality of nature and the world can

142

be found in Justus Buchler's "On the Concept of 'The World,' *Review of Metaphysics*, XXXI/4, June 1978, pp. 555-579, and "Probing the Idea of Nature," *Process Studies*, VIII/3, Fall 1978, pp. 157-68, as well as in my *Transition to an Ordinal Metaphysics* and "The Inexhaustibility of Nature," *Journal of Value Inquiry*, VIII/4, Winter 1973, pp. 241-53. However, in the context of this first chapter, the principle of inexhaustibility should be regarded as one among several competing hypotheses which address the mystery of Being.

4. John Dewey: "The Need for a Recovery of Philosophy," reprinted in *On Experience, Nature and Freedom*, R. Bernstein ed., Indianapolis, Bobbs-Merrill, 1960.

5. Leibniz: *On the Ultimate Origin of Things*.

6. *Ibid.*

II. Some Philosophic Mysteries

1. Alfred North Whitehead: *Science and the Modern World*, New York, Macmillan, 1925, pp. 249-50.

2. Alfred North Whitehead: *Process and Reality*, New York, Macmillan, 1929, p. 106.

3. J. M. E. McTaggart: *The Nature of Existence*, Vol. II, Cambridge, Cambridge University Press, 1927, Ch. 33.

4. Time is mysterious insofar as it is either ultimate or evanescent. Most physical theories of time after Einstein adopt the Minkowskian four-dimensional continuum diagram in which the future is as determinate as the past, a version of McTaggart's earlier-later sequence. The past-present-future sequence is then effectively relegated to consciousness and appearance, and is irrelevant to physical time.

5. George Herbert Mead: *Philosophy of the Present*, La Salle, Ill., Open Court, 1932.

6. Aristotle: *Physics*, II, 6.

7. John Herman Randall Jr.: *Aristotle*, New York, Columbia University Press, 1960, p. 183.

8. Gilbert Ryle: *The Concept of Mind*, London, Hutchinson, 1949.

9. William James: "Does Consciousness Exist?," *Essays in Radical Empiricism*, New York, Longmans, Green, 1912, pp. 3-4.

10. Gilbert Ryle: *The Concept of Mind*, p. 25.

III. God

1. David Hume: *Dialogues on Natural Religion*, Part X.

2. Schubert M. Ogden: "Toward a New Theism," in D. Brown *et al.*, eds., *Process Philosophy and Christian Thought*, Indianapolis, Bobbs-Merrill, 1971.

3. William James: *Varieties of Religious Experience*, New York, Modern Library, 1929, Conclusion.

4. William James: *A Pluralistic Universe*, New York, Longmans, Green, 1909, p. 321.

5. Stephen David Ross: *Transition to an Ordinal Metaphysics*, Chapter VII.

6. See Justus Buchler, *Toward a General Theory of Human Judgment*, and especially *Nature and Judgment*, Chapter II. See also the discussion below, pp. 92-94, 105-118.

IV. Ordinal Pluralism

1. There is some similarity here with Wittgenstein's family theory of meaning, though there is no resolution of the identity of orders in social practice as there is in Wittgenstein's analysis. (Ludwig Wittgenstein: *Philosophical Investigations*, Oxford, Blackwell, 1963.) For this reason, the ordinal theory offers a far more general account of the complementary relationship of determinateness and indeterminateness, and defines the general conditions of mystery in a far more systematic way, than can be found in Wittgenstein's later work.

2. It is also denied by Buchler in *Metaphysics of Natural Complexes*, pp. 60-61.

INDEX

145

149

Relativity, theory of, 37; *See also* Einstein, Science
Relevance, 27, 67-71, 73-74, 76, 90, 99, 104; *See also* Constituent, Irrelevance, Ordinality. Relation; integral and scopic, 69; *See also* Integrity, Scope
Religion, 54-56, 59-65, 109, 119, 137; *See also* God
Responsibility, moral, 32-33; *See also* Morality
Ryle, G., 41-43, 143

Scepticism, 1-2, 8, 96-97, 122, 135-36; *See also* Knowledge, Query
Science, 3, 10, 12, 14, 30, 32, 37-38, 44-45, 47, 50, 54, 60, 62-64, 85-86, 92-94, 106-107, 112-16, 125-27, 129, 132-39; *See also* Assertive judgment, Physical sciences, Query, Social sciences
Scope, 10, 69, 72-74, 82, 87, 89-92, 98-103, 111, 114-16, 129, 131, 133, 135, 139; *See also* Integrity, Ordinality
Self-actualization, 28
Self-causation, 34-35; *See also* Causation
Self-contradiction, 9, 27
Self-evidence, 8-9, 11; *See also* Validation
Self-significance, 83
Simplicity, 69-70, 81, 83; *See also* Inexhaustibility
Social sciences, 1, 3, 106, 109-11, 133, 136-137; *See also* Science
Society, 33, 37, 48-49, 53, 63. 132-40
Sociology, 38, 110; *See also* Social sciences, Society
Solutions, 4-5, 15; *See also* Problems, Query
Space, 19, 84-86, 116
Spatialization, 27; *See also* Space
Spinoza, 10, 13, 17, 40, 58, 98-99
Spontaneity; *See* Arbitrariness, Chance, Freedom, Possibility
Style, 45, 51; *See also* Art
Substance, 17, 40-41
Supernatural. 55, 62; *See also* Divine, God, Religion
Supreme mystery, 25, 37, 54, 61, 132, 136; *See also* Cosmological argument, Ultimacy

Surd, 7, 21; *See also* Unintelligibility
Syndetic judgment, 44-45, 63-65, 94-95, 105, 107, 109-11, 113, 118, 127, 129-30; *See also* Metaphysics, Philosophy
System, 6, 31, 35-38, 115; *See also* Comprehensiveness, Systematic philosophy, Universe, World
Systematic philosophy, 1, 9-12; *See also* Comprehensiveness, Metaphysics, Philosophy

Technology, 3, 50, 133-34, 139; *See also* Science
Teleology, 6; *See also* Causation, final
Theism, 56, 62; *See also* God
Theology, 56, 59, 65; *See also* God, Religion
Thought, 16, 39, 136; *See also* Knowledge, Mind
Tillich, P., 58-59
Time, 13, 25-32, 58, 84-86, 89, 111, 116, 119, 138; *See also* Becoming
Totalitarianism, 48; *See also* Politics
Totality, 6, 16-18, 20, 22-23, 29-30, 57, 69, 76-79, 82, 104, 108; *See also* Comprehensiveness, World
Trait, 33; *See also* Constituent
Transition to an Ordinal Metaphysics, 67, 142-44
Transitivity of relevance, 69, 71, 104, 117; *See also* Relevance
Truth, 9, 38, 44-45, 53, 59, 106-107, 109; *See also* Assertive judgment, Science, Validation
Typicality; *See* Prevalence

Ultimacy, ultimate mysteries, 6-7, 28, 31-32, 56, 60-62, 98-99, 113, 118-21; *See also* God, World
Understanding, 2, 5-6, 8-9, 28-29, 40, 66, 100; *See also* Knowledge, Query, Rationality
Uniqueness, 51, 55, 58; *See also* Integrity
Unitariness, 68; *See also* Integrity
Unity, 109; of the world, 18, 21, 22; *See also* Comprehensiveness, Syndetic judgment

Univalence, 114-16; *See also* Inexhausti-
bility, Plurality, Science
Universe, 6-8, 17-19, 22-23, 25, 31-32,
35, 38, 41, 54, 59, 82, 85, 104, 116,
120, 132; *See also* Nature, World
Unreality, 18; *See also* Ontological parity,
Reality
Unrelatedness, 71; *See also* Irrelevance

Validation, 44-45, 53, 63, 92-94, 106-
112, 118, 122, 125, 128, 136; *See
also* Judgment, Query, Truth
Value, 16, 31-32, 46-53; *See also* Validation

Verifiability principle, 4

Whitehead, 8, 25-26, 83, 142-43
Will, 32, 46-47, 56, 58
Wisdom, J., 2, 142
Wittgenstein, 2, 142, 144
World, 6-7, 13, 17-23, 26, 29-30, 32, 34-
37, 39-40, 42, 49, 54, 56-57, 69-71,
75-76, 81-85, 89, 98-99, 101, 104-105,
119, 122-123, 125, 129, 132, 137; *See
also* Inexhaustibility, Nature
Worship, 56, 62; *See also* God, Religion

Zeno, 25-26

0310